SHONINKI
THE SECRET TEACHINGS
OF THE NINJA

SHONINKI

THE SECRET TEACHINGS OF THE NINJA

The
17th-Century
Manual
on the
Art of
Concealment

MASTER NATORI MASAZUMI
With Commentaries by Axel Mazuer

Translated by Jon E. Graham

Destiny Books
Rochester, Vermont • Toronto, Canada

Destiny Books
One Park Street
Rochester, Vermont 05767
www.DestinyBooks.com

Destiny Books is a division of Inner Traditions International

Originally published in French under the title *Shoninki: L'authentique manuel des ninja* by Éditions Albin Michel, 22, rue Huyghens, 75014 Paris
First U.S. edition published in 2010 by Destiny Books

Library of Congress Cataloging-in-Publication Data

Natori, Masazumi 17th cent.
  [Shoninki. English]
  Shoninki : the secret teachings of the ninja : the 17th-century manual on the art of concealment / Natori Masazumi ; with commentaries by Axel Mazuer ; translated by Jon E. Graham. — 1st U.S. ed.
    p. cm.
  Includes index.
  ISBN 978-1-59477-343-3 (pbk.)
  1. Ninjutsu—Early works to 1800. 2. Espionage—Japan—Early works to 1800. 3. Martial arts—Japan—Early works to 1800. I. Mazuer, Axel. II. Title.
  UB271.J3N37613 2010
  355.5'48—dc22

                                           2010014901

Printed and bound in the United States by Lake Book Manufacturing

10   9   8   7   6   5   4   3   2   1

Text design by Priscilla Baker
Text layout by Virginia Scott Bowman
This book was typeset in Garamond Premier Pro with Albertus and Gill Sans as display typefaces

CONTENTS

PART TWO

Shoninki Shokan: First Scroll of the *Shoninki*

PART THREE

Shoninki Chukan: Middle Scroll of the *Shoninki*

PART FOUR

Shoninki Gekan: Final Scroll of the *Shoninki*

FOREWORD

◄─►

The *Shoninki* is the essential reference work of ninjutsu. In feudal Japan it was even used as a sign of recognition between shinobi (ninja). This is why any person practicing ninjutsu or having any interest in the subject at all should own a copy of this book and refer to it regularly. Not only does this version provide the most trustworthy reference on ninjutsu now available outside of Japan, but it also stands out as the keystone for any library devoted to the martial arts. Beyond that, this book deserves a place of choice in the libraries of all those interested in ancient Japan.

This text by the master ninja of the Kishu School, Natori Masazumi, is his masterpiece, offering readers an unprecedented view of seventeenth-century Japan as seen by one of its essential figures. More than just a practical manual, this book offers testimony from a remote past, from a time and a land where the slightest mistake could mean death. It is like an ancestor to whom we owe the greatest respect. Along with the *Ninpiden,* the *Bansenshukai,* and the *Ninpo Hikan,* it is the progenitor of all books on traditional ninjutsu.

The *Shoninki* advocates detachment, self-esteem, and letting go. As a psychotherapist I cannot help but give my blessing to this undertaking. What's more, it encourages self-knowledge and trust in our own intuition, which meshes perfectly with my own concerns as a Zen practitioner.

The modern reader may not know what good fortune it is that we can hold this book in our hands. After remaining a closely guarded secret for a long time, even in Japan, this ninja "bible" has crossed over ages and continents to make its way to us and surrender its age-old secrets. More importantly, its appearance in the Western world should cast a light that will banish to the shadows a good many mediocre books on this subject written by authors enslaved to sensationalism.

May this book, dear readers, find in your heart the "powerful light" (*daikomyo*) and rekindle it for greater happiness and success in your lives.

BERNARD BORDAS,
BUJINKAN SHIHAN

Bernard Boras was born in 1957 and started to practice the martial arts and combat sports at age eleven. He is the recipient of the title *Shihan* (Master Expert in Japanese martial arts) from the Bujinkan organization, a prestigious martial arts school—particularly of ninjutsu—founded and directed by Master Masaaki Hatsumi. Bordas has devoted his life to the practice of ninjutsu, which he states, "is not only a technique but also a state of mind: survival."

INTRODUCTION

THE CULTURAL AND PHILOSOPHICAL CONTEXT OF THE *SHONINKI*

◄─►

In feudal Japan, the *ninja* were agents employed to perform espionage and guerilla missions. The *Shoninki* (which translates into English as "authentic ninja tradition") is the work of Natori Masazumi, the master ninja who directed the Kishu School (Kishu-ryu) of one of the principal ninja clans in seventeenth-century Japan. For this reason, this short treatise is one of the most important documents on *ninjutsu* (ninja practices). It makes it clear that, far from being restricted to a purely physical teaching, the ninjutsu practice was accompanied by a foundational teaching that was philosophical, even esoteric, in nature, which moves it beyond being simply a set of techniques. It is my intention to provide in this introduction a few of the factors that make it possible to comprehend the doctrines on which the *Shoninki* was based as well as its historical and cultural background.

The regions of Koga and Iga in the area surrounding Lake Biwa (see page 2) were the geographical heart of traditional ninjutsu. They are considered as the birthplace of the *ninpo*

1

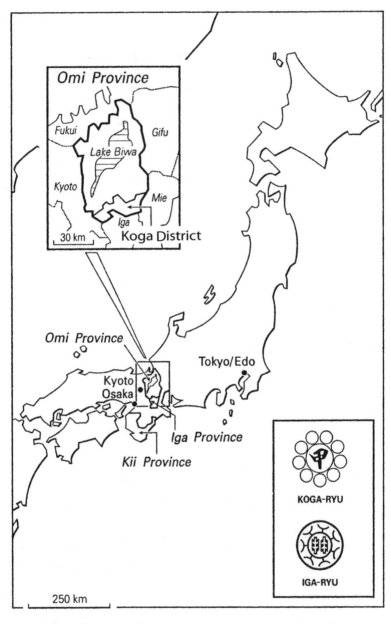

Map of Japan, with ancient ninja areas around Lake Biwa
Inset: Seals of the Koga and Iga Schools

(ninja practices), and the names of the old ninjutsu schools of Iga and Koga (Iga-ryu and Koga-ryu) are still famous today. Today the ancient province of Iga is part of the modern prefecture of Mie, while Koga (an administrative subdivision of the former province of Omi) is part of the modern prefecture of Shiga. The Kishu-ryu school—associated with the former province of Kishu located south of Iga—is sometimes regarded as a derivative branch of the Iga-ryu. Today Kishu corresponds to the prefecture of Wakayama (near Kii peninsula). Geographically, all of the ancient centers connected with the ninja are located in the current region of Kansai (or Kinki).

NINJA: THE HISTORY OF A WORD

The ninja had many different names bestowed upon them in different regions and at different times. The generic terms of *mawashi-mono* (or *kancho-no-mono*), derived from the verb *mawasu,* "to circle around," and *saguri-no-mono,* from the verb *saguru,* "to look for, spy, probe," were used to designate spies. The term *ninja* or *shinobi* (which is a different reading of the same ideograms) was used only in some provinces.

Names of the Ninja in the Various Regions of Feudal Japan

Kyoto/Nara: *suppa* or *seppa, ukami, dakko, shinobi,* or *shinobu*

Aorimi: *hayamchimono, shinobi,* or *shinobu*

Myagi: *kurohabaki*

Kanagawa: *kusa, kamari, monomi, rappa, toppa*

Tokyo/Edo: *onmitsu, oniwaban*

Yamanashi: *mitsumono, suppa* or *seppa, sukinami, denuki*

Aichi: *kyodan*

Fukui: *shinobi* or *shinobu*

Nigata: *nokizura, kyoudou, kyoudan, kikimono-yaku, kanshi,* or *kansha*

Shiga/Koga: *senkunin, senku-no-mono, Koga-no-mono, Koga Shu, ongyo-no-mono*

Mie/Iga: *Iga-no-mono, Iga shu, shinobi-no-mono*

Okayama: *Fuma kainin*

Yamashiro and Yamato: *suppa, dakko, ukami,* or *ukagami*

Kai: *suppa, mitsu-no-mono*

Echigo and Etchu: *nokizaru, kanshi, kikimono-yaku*

Mutsu/Miyagi: *kuro-habaki*

Mutsu/Aomori: *hayamichi-no-mono, shinobi*

Sagami: *kusa, monomi, rappa*

Echizen and Wakasa: *shinobi*

Use of the term *ninja* is relatively modern, as it was made popular during the early 1900s. Before this time the most commonly used name was *shinobi* or *shinobi-no-mono* (furtive individual). *Shinobi* is the word primarily used in the translation of this text. One of the reasons for this choice is that the word *ninjutsu* (or *ninja*) is not as easy to translate as it might appear at first glance. There is little difficulty in determining the right translation for *jutsu* 術, which means "technique," "art," or for *ja* 者, which means "he who," "individual," "person," or "man." However, the *kanji* (Chinese character) *nin* 忍 possesses several distinctly different levels of meaning. At the most elementary level, this word should be understood as meaning "to endure," "tolerate," "undergo," "tenacity," or "endurance." In the next layer of meaning, the sense of this word becomes similar to shinobi: "furtive," "secret," "hidden," or "invisible."

But if the kanji for *nin* is broken down, it is made up of the combination of two different ideograms: the kanji *shin* or *kokoro,* meaning "spirit" or "heart" (in the symbolic sense of "soul," "courage," "will," "feelings," and so forth), is placed underneath the kanji *yaiba,* meaning "blade" (and more specifically the blade of the sword, the saber).

Nin = kokoro and yaiba

Others have taken this analysis even further by breaking the kanji *yaiba* down into its components of *ha* ＼, which means "sting," combined with *to* 刀, which means "sword;" together they mean the "sting of the sword" rather than simply "blade." The result has been a plethora of different interpretations for the meaning of *nin,* which in turn has served as a springboard for finding an equal variety of possible meanings for the word *ninjutsu* or *ninja.*

By definition, *ninjutsu* and *ninja* of course serve as the preeminent terms for the "art of invisibility" and the "furtive individual." As the *Shoninki* indicates (in the third chapter of the *Shoninki Jo*), the ninja is also he who "places his heart beneath the blade of the sword." In other words the ninja is the individual who has to risk his life (especially during a mission), or symbolically the individual who lives with a sword of Damocles hanging above his head—someone in constant danger. He must be tough to endure a situation like this and his furtive nature will allow him to escape danger.

But nin also means "the will that can endure the sting of the sword," thereby making ninjutsu "the way of endurance," whether this endurance is physical, mental, or moral in nature. This means knowing how to endure pain and humiliation (for example, when disguised as a crippled beggar to avoid arousing suspicion); knowing how to be patient enough to remain hidden, motionless for hours; and knowing how to bear suffering, such as holding the pain of an injury in the depths of your heart and hiding it from others in order to fulfill a mission.

But this could also be "the art of the union of the mind with the sword" or "the body and the spirit." This refers to the mind's control over the body, which is the tool to express the mind's pure and flawless will with a terrible efficiency, ready to do whatever proves necessary to achieve its objective. This indicates that ninjutsu, like all the other reputable Japanese martial arts, can also be a Way (*do*) of ultimately seeking the perfect mind/body union. The word *nin* thus also refers to a "tough heart," a patient and tenacious will with the effectiveness of a blade.

Pursuing this direction further, we can also interpret ninjutsu as meaning "the art of one who knows how to use his mind like a weapon," the art of one who triumphs by virtue of his knowledge, experience, and cunning. But it could also be seen as an allusion to "the strength of the will" and "the power of the mind" as parapsychological powers that were goals of ninja training. With respect to its esoteric aspect, ninjutsu could lastly be understood as "art of the hidden mind," "the secrets of the heart," which is to say "of hidden, secret knowledge."

It should be noted that some grand masters, like Master Hatsumi, have objected to the identification of ninjutsu as a *do*, reserving this term instead for the practice of seated meditation (*zazen*).

As we shall read in the first chapters of the *Shoninki,* ninja were also sometimes called *nusubito,* a term used to describe thieves. This was a logical attribution, as the clandestine activities of thief and ninja often intersected. However, *nusubito* is a contemptuous term that is quite pejorative, and the *Shoninki* quickly takes pains to draw a clear distinction between nusubito and authentic ninja, explaining that while thieves (nusubito) can technically behave like ninja to some extent, that does not make them true ninja. The *Shoninki* therefore establishes a clear distinction between ninja and nusubito, even though their spheres of activity clearly overlapped.

THE ORIGIN OF NINJUTSU

It is highly likely that ninjutsu's origin was in China, as explained by the second chapter of the first scroll. The Chinese were quite familiar with spies and had many different names for them, as mentioned in the *Shoninki*: *die (cho)*, *diezhe (chosha)*, *xizuo (saisaku)*, *youzhen (yutei)*, *quianzhen (kentei)*, *jiandie (kancho)*, and *tansi (tanshi)*. More specifically, ancient China also had a technique equivalent to ninjutsu, known under the name of *yin-sen-shu* or *fa-shu*. It is also said that the masters of kung fu *wushu* (martial arts), had to learn *chin kung* in tandem with their training in the "classic" martial arts. *Chin kung* is the art of making light work of obstacles in the same way as the ninja of feudal Japan: scaling a wall like a lizard, walking through the grass (or even the snow!) without leaving any trace, and so forth.*

Similarly, there were several equivalents to the ninja on the Far Eastern continent, mainly in Korea, where they were called *sulsa* (knights of the night) and their art was known under the name of *eunshinbop* or *insul eunshinbop*.

At the very least, it is certain that the construction and development of Japanese ninjutsu benefited from the knowledge contributed by Chinese exiles, both on the technical plane as well as on the philosophical or strategic plane. Specifically, there are references to Sun Tzu's *The Art of War* and the *Wu xing*, teachings regarding the five elements.

Types of Spies from The Art of War

The Art of War, which dates back to around 500 BCE, is probably the first treatise on strategy ever written. Its influence on ninjutsu is undeniable. The *Shoninki* picked up the typology of the five types of Chinese spies from which the ninja originated, developed by Sun Tzu in the chapter (XIII or XII, depending on the different editions) concerning secret

---

*Dr. Leung Ting has written a very interesting book on the Chinese roots of ninpo, available in English with the title *Skills of the Vagabonds: From Where the Japanese Ninjutsu Originated,* vol. 1 (Hong Kong: Leung Ting Co, 1988).

agents.* The *Shoninki* was inspired specifically by paragraphs five to eleven. Here is the text (as translated by Lionel Giles):

XIII. The Use of Spies

1. Sun Tzu said: Raising a host of a hundred thousand men and marching them great distances entails heavy loss on the people and a drain on the resources of the State. The daily expenditure will amount to a thousand ounces of silver. There will be commotion at home and abroad, and men will drop down exhausted on the highways. As many as seven hundred thousand families will be impeded in their labor.

2. Hostile armies may face each other for years, striving for the victory which is decided in a single day. This being so, to remain in ignorance of the enemy's condition simply because one grudges the outlay of a hundred ounces of silver in honors and emoluments, is the height of inhumanity.

3. One who acts thus is no leader of men, no present help to his sovereign, no master of victory.

4. Thus, what enables the wise sovereign and the good general to strike and conquer, and achieve things beyond the reach of ordinary men, is foreknowledge.

5. Now this foreknowledge cannot be elicited from spirits; it cannot be obtained inductively from experience, nor by any deductive calculation.

6. Knowledge of the enemy's dispositions can only be obtained from other men.

---

*Anyone seeking to get a better grasp of the overall question of strategy would be well advised to accompany the reading of Sun Tzu's *The Art of War* with that of *The Thirty-Six Strategies,* attributed to the same author in error by many historians. Several editions of this work are available.

7. Hence the use of spies, of whom there are five classes: (1) local spies; (2) inward spies; (3) converted spies; (4) doomed spies; (5) surviving spies.*

8. When these five kinds of spy are all at work, none can discover the secret system. This is called "divine manipulation of the threads." It is the sovereign's most precious faculty.

9. Having local spies means employing the services of the inhabitants of a district.

10. Having inward spies, making use of officials of the enemy.

11. Having converted spies, getting hold of the enemy's spies and using them for our own purposes.

12. Having doomed spies, doing certain things openly for purposes of deception, and allowing our spies to know of them and report them to the enemy.

13. Surviving spies, finally, are those who bring back news from the enemy's camp.

14. Hence it is that in the whole army no more intimate relations are to be maintained than with spies. None should be more liberally rewarded. In no other business should greater secrecy be preserved.

15. Spies cannot be usefully employed without a certain intuitive sagacity.

16. They cannot be properly managed without benevolence and straightforwardness.

---

*A number of varied terms exist in translation for these five types of spies or secret agents. For example, "indigenous agents" is sometimes used for local spies; "interior agents or spies" or "infiltrated agents" for *inward spies;* "turned agents" or "double agents" for *converted spies;* "dead agents," "spies that can be liquidated," or "sacrificed agents" for *doomed spies;* and "living agents," "flying agents," or "reusable agents" for *surviving spies.*

17. Without subtle ingenuity of mind, one cannot make certain of the truth of their reports.

18. Be subtle! be subtle! and use your spies for every kind of business.

19. If a secret piece of news is divulged by a spy before the time is ripe, he must be put to death together with the man to whom the secret was told.

20. Whether the object be to crush an army, to storm a city, or to assassinate an individual, it is always necessary to begin by finding out the names of the attendants, the aides-de-camp, and door-keepers and sentries of the general in command. Our spies must be commissioned to ascertain these.

21. The enemy's spies who have come to spy on us must be sought out, tempted with bribes, led away, and comfortably housed. Thus they will become converted spies and available for our service.

22. It is through the information brought by the converted spy that we are able to acquire and employ local and inward spies.

23. It is owing to his information, again, that we can cause the doomed spy to carry false tidings to the enemy.

24. Lastly, it is by his information that the surviving spy can be used on appointed occasions.

25. The end and aim of spying in all its five varieties is knowledge of the enemy; and this knowledge can only be derived, in the first instance, from the converted spy. Hence it is essential that the converted spy be treated with the utmost liberality.

26. Of old, the rise of the Yin dynasty was due to I Chih who had served under the Hsia. Likewise, the rise of the

Chou dynasty was due to Lu Ya who had served under the Yin.

27. Hence it is only the enlightened ruler and the wise general who will use the highest intelligence of the army for purposes of spying and thereby they achieve great results. Spies are a most important element in war, because on them depends an army's ability to move.*

In addition to the passage in the *Shoninki*, the first volume of the *Bansenshukai* (another classic of the ninja tradition) also refers to *The Art of War* specifically by name.

The Five-Elements Principle in China and Japan

The "principle of the five elements" that appears in the final scroll of the *Shoninki* has its origin in what is referred to in Chinese as *Wu xing,* an abbreviated form of *Wu zhong liu xing zhi chi,* meaning "the five types of chi that are dominant at different times."

The curves that make up the circle connecting the five elements (see page 13) represent the "cycle of generation" (*In yo so sei* in Japanese): wood produces fire (the log burns); fire produces earth (in the form of powdered ash); earth produces metal (mineral extracts that form in the soil); metal produces water (by liquefying when it is melted); and water produces wood (by causing trees and other vegetation to grow). In the same figure the straight lines forming the star connecting the five elements represent the "cycle of destruc-

---

Sun Tzu on the Art of War, the Oldest Military Treatise in the World, translated from the Chinese by Lionel Giles, 1910 (which can be accessed at www.chinapage.com/sunzi-e.html).

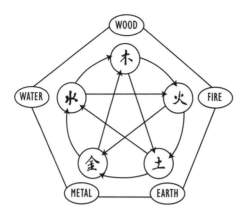

The cycles of generation and destruction of the five elements

tion or domination" (*In yo sokuiko* in Japanese): water extinguishes fire; fire melts metal; metal cuts wood; wood covers the earth (by growing in the form of trees); and the earth absorbs water.

In addition to this there is a large play of rich symbolic correspondences between the Chinese Wu xing and the five fundamental emotions, the five yang organs of the human body, the five senses, the five stages of life, the five seasons of the year (for the Chinese), the times of the day, the five animals of Shaolin King Fu or therapeutic Qi Gong, the sounds, the colors, and so on.

Engendered by the ancient *I Ching* (The Book of Changes), the Wu xing was developed in China around the end of the fifth century CE. It next moved into Japan, where it took the name of *gogyo*. In tandem with the gogyo that emerged out of Chinese Taoism, Buddhism crafted its own version of this "five-elements principle," the *godai*, with several variations and adaptations.

The Buddhist godai is slightly distinguished from the Chinese Wu xing and the Japanese gyogo by the fact that the elements of wood or metal are replaced by the void or the wind (air) depending on the variant version. Its cycle also begins with the element earth in contrast to gyogo, which systematically opens with the element wood. Godai was later incorporated by the esoteric branch of Buddhism in Japan during the tenth century CE under the name of *gorin* (the "five wheels" or the "five rings"). From there, godai and gorin eventually moved into ninjutsu, where this principle of the five elements became an essential aspect of the esoteric ninja teaching (the *ninpo-mikkyo*).

The Influence of the Five Elements on Combat Techniques

At a primary level, the five wheels gave structure to all the ninja combat techniques. The majority of Japanese martial arts, especially samurai training, were based on a collective mass teaching, in which the student received extensive drilling in a combat technique that basically remained foreign to his personality. Ninjutsu used the opposite approach: the students were given individual instruction, taught in very small groups in a way that followed their natural inclinations. Consequently, there were no preestablished technical programs (*katas*). Instead, combat techniques, both armed and weaponless, defensive and offensive moves, positions, and so on were simply classified into broad categories, coded by one of the five natural elements as a symbol of certain tendencies, such as fire for offensive and explosive, water for defensive and fluid, and so forth. These tendencies were adopted by an individual ninja during combat based on circumstances, his morphology, his state of mind at the time, and the adversary he was facing.

The apprentice ninja was therefore not expected to learn all the movements in each category but simply to select over the course of his training the defensive and offensive moves that were most instinctive for him and which best responded to his nature. This guaranteed that the acquisition and development of his fighting technique would be as specifically personal and available as his own personality. As a result, his technique would always be unpredictable. This variation of technique from one ninja to the next offered no reference point for an adversary that would allow him to identify a particular style, therefore making it more difficult for him to perfect any countertechniques.

This is the reason that the style of ninja combat frequently gave observers the characteristic impression of a certain "natural dynamic." Recognizable here is the "libertarian" mentality of the ninja art at its origins, underscoring individuality (in contrast to the hierarchical respect of the castes so distinctive of the samurai), and ensuring that the system adapted to the student instead of obliging the student to conform to a system.

On a strategic level, gygyo/gorin also helped to classify the techniques of evasion (*in-ton*), camouflage, and flight, which were known as *gotonpo*. Hiding oneself, thanks to the earth, was known as *dotonjutsu* (hiding behind a rock or in a camouflaged ditch or crevice in the rock, covering oneself with a thin layer of dirt). Other concealment techniques were also classified in accordance with the elements: hiding thanks to wood or *mokutonjutsu* (climbing and concealing oneself in the trees, hiding behind bushes, or crawling through the grass, and so on); hiding by virtue of water or *suitonjutsu;* hiding thanks to fire or *katonjutsu* (using smoke bombs, starting a fire to create a diversion, and so on), and hiding thanks to metal or *kintonjutsu* (creating a diversion by throwing a metal object whose noise diverts a sentry's attention, throwing caltrops to hamper the progress of a pursuer when making an escape, using various ordinary objects made of metal to hide oneself, and so forth).

In the first scroll of the *Shoninki,* the chapter dedicated to the "meditations on water birds" makes an allusion to this principle of adapting and merging with the elements in order to hide: "Spying means blending in with the widest variety of things and in this way concealing yourself skillfully and with art."

The Five Elements and Meditation

Finally, on the spiritual and esoteric level, gorin played an important role in meditation techniques. Each element represented a type of "energy" or state of mind. In the performance of mudras, magic gestures made with the fingers, each of the five fingers corresponded with one of the elements (in order from the little finger to the thumb: earth, water, fire, wind, and the void).

We should also note that the five magical spells mentioned in chapter 5 of the middle scroll also arose from this Chinese five-elements principle.

THE CONTRIBUTION OF OTHER FORMS OF TRADITIONAL KNOWLEDGE

The *Shoninki* relies on other forms of traditional knowledge as well, such as face reading, astrology, and traditional astronomy.

Chapters 9 and 10 of the middle scroll of the *Shoninki* are dedicated to physiognomy, the art of reading the personality and destiny of a person through their outer appearance, particularly their facial features. This doctrine seems to have held a very large influence in medieval Japan.*

During the Edo era, a physiognomy book of Chinese origin, the *Nanboku Sobo,* enjoyed great and widespread success in Japan. This work distinguishes between three parts of the face: the upper part, related to intelligence and the first years of life; the middle part, related to feelings and maturity; and finally the lower part, which refers to the instincts and the end of life. Although these distinctions established by the *Nanboku Sobo* do not correspond exactly with those in the *Shoninki,* it seems to have had some influence on the writing of the latter book.

Incidentally, the conclusion of chapter 10 of the middle

---

*Some of the details of this doctrine may appear naïve or comical to many modern readers, but do not be too quick to laugh. We should recall that during this same time period in Europe numerous Western grimoires like the *Great or Little Albert* often provided similar treatises on physiognomy, which were frequently inspired by older treatises written by Greek and Roman authors. Without them the physiognomic doctrine (and its derivatives like phrenology) would never have enjoyed such success in nineteenth-century Europe, as demonstrated by the popularity of such books as Johann Kaspar Lavater's *The Art of Knowing Men through Physiognomy* (1820) and Cesare Lombroso's *The Criminal Man* (1887).

scroll of the *Shoninki* tempers and takes a certain distance from the precepts of face reading: "The purpose of these notes is to draw up an inventory of characteristics bestowed by birth. Yet, sometimes mistakes have been made. Although, for example, a person's character may appear completely evil, it can happen that he has some good aspects and should not be stigmatized because of some bad character features. Predicting the good and evil in an individual is a difficult undertaking that must be approached with finesse."

What should be held most firmly in mind from these chapters is the principle explained in their introduction: "There are methods for observing people that will allow you to indubitably recognize how they think as well as their character. It is said that the Self listens to the heart attentively, so observing the heart allows you to see and read that of the other like your own image in a mirror. He whose heart is not serene can quickly fall victim to others. This is why the shinobi uses this technique and is able to follow his adversary's heart anywhere and penetrate it."

In fact, the short treatise on physiognomy that brings the middle scroll to a close is but a preliminary sketch introducing the final scroll of the *Shoninki,* which develops the technique of observation far more extensively.

ESOTERIC TECHNIQUES AND SPIRITUALITY

The *Shoninki* suggests the existence of a connection between ninja and *yamabushi.* Also known as *shugenja, genja,* or *genza,* the yamabushi were first and foremost dissident mystics, who lived in the mountains for the most part, which earned them their name. *Yamabushi* is written in Japanese as: 山 武 士. While most Western books translate it as "warrior (*bushi*) of the mountains (*yama*)," this is not at all correct! To be exact, *yamabushi* actually means "those who prostrate themselves" or "those who lie down" on the mountain. While *yama*: 山 does in fact mean "mountain," the mistake in the standard translation stems from the verb *fusu*: 伏, which means "to prostrate oneself, hide, lie down." The noun derived from *fusu* is *fushi;* when it occurs as the second half of a compound word formed with *yama,* the *f* is turned into a *b,* thus creating yamabushi, which is written like this: 山 伏.

To confuse things even more, the word *yamabushi* is very close phonetically to *yamaboshi*: 山 法 師 or *yama-hoshi,* used to designate warrior monks, the "monks (*hoshi*) of the mountain." These monks were the Buddhist monks of Mount Hiei, more specifically those of Enryaku-ji Temple located on that mountain. These monk-warriors were customarily called *hoshi-musha* (monk-warriors), *akuso* (formidable or ferocious monks), or even, in the historical texts written during the Edo period, *sohei* (soldier-monks).

Actually, the yamabushi were adepts of the esoteric doctrines of Buddhism such as *Shingon* or *Tendai,* and practitioners of *shugendo* (path of practical exercises for obtaining psychic powers). Folk tradition cast them in the role of powerful magicians and the keepers of occult traditions who were endowed with supernatural powers. They sought to acquire these powers through ascetic practices and meditation, as well as sometimes through the martial arts. They were often identified with the *tengu* (mountain spirits who were half man and half crow), either serving as their privileged intermediaries or simply considered to be one and the same.

Greatly influenced by its initial cohabitation with the yamabushi, ninjutsu is rich with numerous magical elements and practices whose purpose is the acquisition of psychic powers. While the influence of shugendo on ninjutsu is still controversial, it is certain that the first ninja communities partially integrated elements from Buddhism's esoteric legacy, as the *Shoninki* mentions. The esoteric teaching of the ninja (*ninpo-mikkyo*) mainly consists of the practice of *mantras* (the vocalization of magic words and sounds) and *mudras* (magic gestures). The *Shoninki* devotes the fifth chapter of the middle scroll ("Secret Teachings for Sowing Dismay in Assassins") to these practices.

The five columns of symbols cited by the *Shoninki* in "Secret Teachings for Sowing Dismay in Assassins" (page 98) are magic spells. It should be noted that some of these signs do not exist in the Japanese common tongue. They are adaptations of magic Chinese spells out of the Wu xing and Taoism. As indicated in the accompanying text, the first two spells are more akin to charms for blessing and protection, while the other three are curses to be directed toward a potential foe.

The *Shoninki* makes no mention of this but for good measure the ultimate implementation of these symbols is to write these magic spells with your own blood.

It may also be noted that four of the spells all share the concluding phrase 急 急 如 律 令 (*kyukyu nyo ritsuryo*), which was used during the Han Dynasty in all official documents as well as in Taoist magic spells. It means: "May my command be carried out at once!" In Japan this phrase was used by the yamabushi during exorcism rites or for divinatory purposes when seeking to predict the outcome of a battle or to determine the most propitious day for victory. It was also used to dispel evil spirits before a battle.

We should also note the presence in three of these spells of a symbol depicting a nine-line grid, referring to the magic number nine, mainly that of the *ninpo kuji-goshin-ho,* a specific sequence of nine different ways of interlacing the fingers, each accompanied by a specific mantra. There were a large number of such mudras (magic gestures formed by the fingers), used for a wide variety of purposes. For example, as a complement to the training of *ankokutoshijutsu* (technique for seeing in the night) there was a mudra spell that was specifically intended to let its caster see better in the dark. Naturally reserved for the ninja initiates, all these magic elements were "unknown to common mortals," as stipulated by the *Shoninki.*

We also can find more specifically Buddhist and even Zen teachings in this book. For example, in the eighth chapter of the middle scroll, it is explained that it is necessary to be "empty," in other words impartial and freed from the ego, with complete absence of self-attachment. As a ninja was adept at worming information from an adversary by flattering his vanity and stroking his ego, if he was himself liberated from this weakness he would be that much more effective: "This is why it is so important to be able to leave your ego to the side."

I have mentioned some of the traditional and esoteric elements found in ninjutsu for the reason that so few readers are aware of them, but their role in the *Shoninki* should not be overestimated. This book is first and foremost a collection of practical techniques (techniques for gathering information, the use of various materials, gaining knowledge of the environment, and so forth), as well as an explication of the psychological and spiritual aspects that the authentic art of ninjutsu assumes will be employed in the implementation of these techniques.

On the broadest scale, ninjutsu shares the same fundamental goal of Zen Buddhism and the majority of the traditional martial arts: "Struggle against the ego in order to obtain awakening as well as a state of inner emptiness, the source of superior effectiveness."

AXEL MAZUER

SHONINKI

PART ONE

Shoninki Jo

INTRODUCTION
TO THE *SHONINKI*

FOREWORD

This book is an examination of the ancient traditions of ninjutsu and the art of the shinobi, which has long existed. More than that, it is a practical manual for military experts, discussing attack and retreat, advantage and disadvantage. The strategies presented in great depth here are both the gate and the key. Every warrior should carefully learn them and become immersed in these precepts.

Thanks to this knowledge, it is possible to assume a position of dominance during dangerous times when reality can be turned upside down with the snap of a finger. Nothing is too difficult for the warrior who employs these strategies, even when he is subject to interrogation by enemy soldiers. He will be able to escape them even if he is not a particularly distinguished soldier, by relying on strategies that are centered on the possession of an unflappable heart.

It is for this reason that people who are too young should not be recruited. If such people are chosen it is as if you are replenishing your enemy's forces with your own soldiers; it is like giving food to a thief. This is why it is very important to be quite judicious in the selection of your people.

By using the secret methods of ninjutsu (such as those

written about by Fujinoisshuishi Masatake), it is possible to confidently take advantage of a skilled warrior versed in numerous arts. Similarly, you can easily draw up a plan against the enemy who guides his life using his own rudder. These resemble the strategies of the yamabushi who conceal themselves in the night. This book itself was once completed and published by hidden and scarcely visible means.

Although the knowledge of ninjutsu may appear superficial and contradictory, it is far from being so. I am merely someone who has extended one part of the path. So it now seems unnecessary for me to waste any more time speaking on this subject.

KATSUDA, CIVIL SERVANT OF KISHU PROVINCE,
WRITTEN DURING THE NINTH YEAR OF THE ENPO ERA,*
DURING THE WAXING MOON AT THE BEGINNING OF AUTUMN

---

*This would be 1681, as the Enpo Era lasted nine years, from 1673 to 1681.

1

THE AUTHENTIC NINJA TRADITION OF OUR SCHOOL

(*TORYU SHONINKI*)

━━◄►━━

Although ninjutsu has existed in Japan since ancient times, it was revealed openly for the first time during the Gempei War,* when Minamoto no Kuro Yoshitsune selected valiant warriors to employ during the battle as shinobi. During the Kemmu era, ninjutsu was used countless times by Kusunoki Masahige.†

Among recent generations, Hojo Ujiyasu‡ employed the

---

*The Gempei War was an important civil war in Japan that lasted from 1180 to 1185. It owes its name to the contraction of the name of its two opposing clans: the Minamoto (or Genji) and the Taira (or Heike). It ended with the victory of the Minamoto clan. Minamoto no Kuro Yoshitsune was one of this clan's most famous warriors. As it happens, this soldier was reputed to possess ninja teachings. It has also been established that his most faithful companion, Saito Musashi-bo Benkei, was a yamabushi.

†Also known as the "Kemmu Restoration," this period encompasses the years 1333 to 1336. Kusunoki Masahige was a samurai who lived from 1294 to 1336 and fought for the emperor Go-Daigo during this period.

‡Lord Hojo Ujiyasu, third representative of the Hojo clan, lived from 1515 to 1571.

nusubito Kazama* to go to different spots in various provinces and investigate certain matters. Takeda Shingen of Kai province† employed people called *suppa*. These individuals were also nusubito of this province.

Eventually this knowledge reached the Koga and Iga regions. From there, ninjutsu next expanded into other provinces until it became known throughout the country. As members of this group, we have exchanged a promise of universal scope. This is why we lend our assistance when a shinobi comes from another province.‡

If I visit another province, the person living in the area will show me his province. If this person visits my province, I will show him the secrets of the area and reveal to him the secrets of my house, thereby putting the marvelous doctrines of this method to work. May the value of this art be recognized!

However, as different generations who meet do not recognize each other with certainty, there is only a single torch inside our house.§ If anyone is seeking to prove his identity, let him brandish this torch and all doubts shall be dispelled.

---

*Kazama is the name of Fuma Kotaro, a ninja from the Fuma clan who worked for the Hojo clan. The exact dates of his birth and death are unknown.

†Takeda Shingen, lord of Shinano and Kai provinces, lived from 1521 to 1573. Like Hojo Ujiyasu, he was one of the principal lords fighting for control over Japan during the sixteenth century.

‡This promise of mutual aid was only valid between members of the Kishu-ryu clan who had swarmed across the land. As a general rule, the ferocious rivalry and quarrels between the different ninja clans (and more widely the various martial arts schools) were proverbial.

§It seems that this "torch" of the Kishu school was nothing other than the *Shoninki,* or at least the oral teachings recorded in it.

Furthermore, the Shoninki is a ninja tradition archive and a family secret. In order to help the expansion of ninjutsu, this generation shall become the transmission center for several shinobi families. Today the ninja tradition is passed on through the Shoninki. Although similar archives exist in other areas, this tradition is the true path of a shinobi from our school.

2

THE DIFFERENT TYPES OF SPIES

(*SHINOBI NO TSUWAMONO NO SHINA*)

The designation of five kinds of spies—local agents, interior agents, double agents, sacrificed agents, and reusable agents—came from China and has been continued in Japan, where the word *gokan* (or *tokan*) is used to describe them. The principle remains the same whatever term is used.

He who can penetrate the essence of these different types and act independently is called a shinobi. When two or three act together as a group, they are called *sonin*. Today, inexperienced young people are employed in groups of two or three. But this is not satisfactory. Caution is advisable when dealing with anyone who is not a specialist. It is preferable, even among experienced warriors, to allow them to operate individually because there have been problems in the past when shinobi have worked as a group. Knowing how to direct an army takes great skill.

CHINESE SPIES

It is said that the shinobi originated in China and that their art was first revealed during the reign of the Yellow Emperor.[*] In an old Chinese scripture (*Saden*[†]), the shinobi were called *cho*. Later they were also called *saisaku*. Tradition maintains that a person in the service of the king of To secretly introduced himself into the home of the king of Jo and killed him.[‡] It is also said that Son Bu,[§] a servitor of the king of Wu, employed five different kinds of information-gathering agents for planning an attack against the enemy.

---

[*]This was the Chinese emperor Huang Di (known as Kotei in Japan), said to have reigned from 2967 to 2598 BCE according to Sima Qian's *Historical Memoirs*. In China he is one of the five mythical emperors of antiquity and is considered to be the father of Chinese civilization.

[†]This refers to a classic Chinese text, the *Zuo zhuan* or *Chuqin Zuoshizhuan* (*Master Zuo's Commentary on the Annals of Spring and Fall of Lu*) written by Zuo Qiuming. It takes the form of a commentary on the *Chunqiu,* the chronicle of the State of Lu (today the province of Shandong), attributed to Confucius. This text describes the events occurring in this state between 722 and 481 BCE. However the *Zuo zhuan* goes beyond mere commentary to depict a longer historical period than the *Chunqiu* (until 468 BCE). In Japanese, the translation of this book is known as the *Saden* or the *Senju Sahiden.*

[‡]Concerning this individual in the king of To's service, tradition maintains that it was Yi Zhi, better known as Yi Yin, who worked for Cheng Tang (founder of the Shang Dynasty). There is apparently some confusion on the part of the Japanese author of the *Shoninki* concerning the assassination of the king of Jo. Historically the "king of Jo" designates the emperor Chu (or Zhou Xin of the Shang Dynasty), but it was Emperor Kestsu, the king of Jie (Jie Gui), the very last emperor of the Ka (or Xia) Dynasty, who was murdered for the benefit of Cheng Tang. One interesting thing about this case of mistaken identity, though, is that both these Chinese emperors were renowned for their cruelty.

[§]This is to say Sun Wu, who has come down to posterity under the name of Sun Tzu or Sun Zi, author of *The Art of War.*

The five types of Chinese spies are:

1. Local agents (*inko no kan*)

   These are trustworthy individuals, able to speak the enemy's language who gather information by carefully eavesdropping on conversations. They resemble the Japanese *dakkonin*.*

2. Interior Agents (*nairyo no kan*)

   These are enemy bureaucrats who can be won to your cause. Their work is of great importance. Because the enemy also employs officials like this, it is important to clearly master the recruitment and use of false spies. This method is also used in Japan, so discretion and caution are constantly required.

3. Double Agents (*hantoku no kan*)

   These are enemy agents that are used like your own agents. These enemy shinobi are treated magnificently like friends. In Japan they are known as *kaerinin* or *sorinin*. If a deeply planted individual of this type is provided with false information, he or she will spread it wherever possible. They can be counted on to see that this information soon becomes common knowledge.

   The means by which the intentions of these agents are penetrated is only transmitted orally (*okuden*).

---

*As mentioned earlier, *dakko* was the name for ninja in the provinces of Yamashiro and Yamato.

4. Sacrificed Agents* (*shicho no kan*)

    These are people who feel very grateful toward you and to whom you give useless information.

5. Reusable Agents (*tensei no kan*)

    These are individuals capable of easily entering enemy territory secretly and who always return with information.

OTHER METHODS OF USING SPIES

The Use of Local Contacts

To easily gain access to desired information about a targeted province, the technique of talking to the local residents *(kyodo)* is used. The best thing is to make friends with the local inhabitants and maintain contact with the common folk. It is also possible to interrogate the inhabitants of the villages when venturing into unknown territories.

It is said, in this regard, that long ago, Sasaki Saburo Moritsuna interrogated two men who lived near a cove and they told him about a shallow spot where he could cross the river. He gave them a *shirasayamaki* sword to express his gratitude. This technique is known as "employing *kyodo.*"

---

*The corresponding kanji means "death." Given the context, the term "sacrificed" seems to be an appropriate and correct translation. This technique of using "sacrificed agents" formed part of ninjutsu under the name of *hotarubi-no-jutsu.* A variation of this technique was called *tensui-no-jutsu.* This came into play when an adversary ninja was unmasked but not arrested. Instead, he was supplied with false or useless information that would serve to lead his master astray.

The Use of "Listening Posts" (gaibun *or* sotogaki)

This method consists of having people outside enemy territory collect important information without sending them to infiltrate deeply into the region. It is possible to obtain information about an enemy territory without even entering it, simply by listening carefully.

While using this method it is extremely important to not trust false rumors and to be quite capable of evaluating people correctly as well as properly analyzing the information collected.

The Ninja or Shinobi-no-mono

Ninja is the Japanese variant of *jianzhe* (*kanja*). A shinobi operates by night or day and never complains of any hardships. He resembles a nusubito but a shinobi does not steal. Individuals like this who easily gather information in even hard-to-reach places and can make their way back without problem from even roadless territories are masters of the art of espionage. They possess the most highly developed skills.

Thieves (nusubito)

Nusubito are devoid of all moral standards and incapable of distinguishing right from wrong. They are indiscreet. For example, like predatory individuals hunting game, they scorn all the boundaries erected by gamekeepers to protect certain reserves and they show no respect for life when they steal from a place. They should be considered as no more than individuals who possess petty skills.

3

THE SUPREME PRINCIPLES OF THE ART OF SHINOBI

(*ICHIRYU NO SHIDAI*)

————◄►————

The Master says: "The work of a shinobi takes him to the very borders of what an individual can tolerate and it is only by exerting much effort that he is able to support it. These highly skilled individuals have to bear in mind when leaving their homes that they will never see those they love or their children again. Whoever returns home can rejoice for escaping his destiny. The shinobi places his heart beneath the blade of a sword.* Similarly, while many people believe that ninjutsu depends on magic, that is not exactly true. Ninjutsu is a practical art and not the imposture of a charlatan."

This is when the disciple asks: "If one listens to the wind blowing, he hears that the art of the shinobi allows him to travel through inaccessible provinces and to soar over frontiers and customs posts that cannot be crossed. He hears that fathers and brothers are no longer able to recognize their own relatives who have become shinobi. Couldn't the use of

———

*See introduction, page 5.

this art—such as when a man, for example, is convinced that someone is standing right in front of him, then suddenly feels the presence of someone at his back, only to turn and see that what he sensed has vanished—be compared to a mysterious rarity, linked to no other tradition? Isn't this the art of practicing complete self-effacement when approaching people to glean information from them?"

The Master answers: "If a person follows a crude principle or an art of little refinement, then that person shall surely make mistakes. But the correct path is marvelous. There are times when a shinobi recognizes reality with his heart, wraps it in a cloak of illusion (or non-reality) and presents it as reality. An experienced shinobi will recognize when an adversary is using the same principle and recognize the reality of the illusion.

"When necessary, the shinobi will also be able to speak the language of a province. He will be able to speak enthusiastically about a place's quality of life, make friends of the inhabitants of a foreign location, and obtain things without spending much money. He will be able to get what he needs to eat and drink, and not become drunk.

"Similarly, the art of the shinobi consists of learning tricks that can be used at critical moments, such as being able to disguise himself as a priest, a wandering monk, a woman, or a girl of the mountains, and, hidden in the night, perform espionage. He should not come down to stay in inns but sleep in open fields with no fear of wild animals in rut. Or else he should be able to flee into the depths of the forest using only the clarity offered by the wonderful light of the moon. A shinobi feels a certain kind of sorrow because of what he has to face and the tricks he uses, but this is something he should never reveal to anyone. There is nothing extraordinary in all of this and the person questioned about it by ordinary folk answers that he is just as ordinary and nothing more. But this is also part of the shinobi's strategy.

"The illusion that has become reality belongs to the real. A shinobi should achieve his goal at the price of hard work and, if at times he strays along the way or his duty blinds his heart, he should never forget the principle of our school."

PART TWO

Shoninki Shokan

FIRST SCROLL
OF THE *SHONINKI*

1

PREPARING YOURSELF FOR CLANDESTINE ACTIVITIES

(*SHINOBI DETACHI JNO NARAI*)

————◄►————

T he foundation of all covert activities is the ability to escape the eyes of others. There are various methods in this regard for hiding your true identity when in the presence of the enemy. Formerly, wise spies could even conceal their identity from members of their own families, from their fathers and children, not to mention their remote relatives.

THE SIX TOOLS

Basically six different tools are used for conducting clandestine activities: a straw hat (*amigasa*), a rope with a hook attached to one end (*kaginawa*), stones for engraving (*sekibitsu*), medicine (*kusuri*), a piece of cloth (*san shaku tenugi*), and material for making fire (*tusketake*). The details concerning the use of these tools are transmitted secretly (*okuden*).

Thanks to the amigasa* it is easy to hide your face and

---

*The *amigasa* is a large basket-shaped straw hat that conceals much of the face.

transform your profile. It is very easy to observe people from underneath your amigasa.

The kaginawa* is used for climbing up to high places, or for rappelling down from them. It can also be used to tie someone up, to lock a door shut, and for many other uses. In our school, the use of the kaginawa for covert activity is a secret field. It can also be used to make a saddle (*kurakatame*).

The sekibitsu is a stone used for writing notes or observations on it with red or black clay; kusuri† is a medicine. You should have these in order to make sure clandestine operations are carried out successfully when crossing through a vast space.

The san shaku tenugi‡ is a piece of cloth used to conceal

---

*The *kagninawa* is a grapple in its most elementary form: a rope (*nawa*) with a hook (*kagi*) attached to one end. The kaginawa had many uses. Like the majority of ninja instruments, it was both a tool and a weapon. But it could also be used for many other things: for fastening on and boarding a boat during a maritime operation (a technique inherited from pirates), for snaring small game, for fishing, and so forth. So it is not surprising that a ninja school considered the particulars of its use to be a "secret field."

†*Kusuri* was rather like the ninja's medicine kit in the form of a *kusuribin,* a small pot or piece of hollow bamboo with one end corked, which was used to carry medicinal substances. It could hold nutritive pills, medicinal remedies, or even poisons.

‡As its name indicates, the *san shaku tenugi* was a piece of cloth three (san) shaku long. A *shaku* was an old Japanese unit of measurement used until 1921. It corresponds to 30.3036 cm (the equivalent of our Western foot). It continues to be used in Japan today to measure the size of swords and bows. The tenugi therefore was almost a yard long. A traditional means of covering the head, it was primarily used by a shinobi to cover his head and face in such a way as to conceal his identity. But it could also be used for other purposes: tying up or gagging a foe, as a filter for dirty water before drinking it, rolled up as a scarf against the cold, muffling the sounds of footsteps by being unrolled on the ground and walked on, and so forth.

the face or worn as a headband (*hachimaki*). It can also be used like a belt or for scaling walls. It has many uses. It is customarily worn beneath the belt folded in half. However, in our school, we fold it and insert it inside the back of the collar. It can also be folded up and inserted it into a *katabira* (light summer garb) but care must be taken so that it does not come undone and fall out.

The tsuketake is used to make fire. It is also very good for making a *kairo*.* It can be used to start a campfire during the night or for lighting the way. Depending on your needs, it could also be used for arson or to set fire to a field.

Additionally, the clothes you wear should be brown, black, or dark blue. The environment can assume the most varied appearances and you should choose the most appropriate color in order to blend in with it. Clothing like a raincoat (*ama-baori*) or a cape (*kappa*) will allow you to skillfully alter your appearance. During secret missions it is advantageous to carry a short sword (*wakizashi*). Ink can also be applied lightly to the scabbard's skin to make it darker. The belt [of the sword] should be black, without any blind stitching. If needed, it can be particularly effective as a quick means of tying things.

---

*The *kairo* was a kind of portable hot water bottle.

THE SEVEN DISGUISES

There are seven ways to disguise oneself (*shushibo no kato*):

1. Itinerant monk (*komuso**): this is when wearing the *amigasa*
2. Buddhist monk (*shukke*): for getting close to people
3. Mountain ascetic (*yamabushi*): for approaching people and carrying a *katana* or a wakizashi[†]
4. Merchant (*akindo*): for freely mingling with people
5. Itinerant actor (*hokashi*): for blending into the crowd
6. Street entertainer (*sarrugaku*): for the same reasons as above
7. Normal appearance[‡] (*tsune kata*): taking on an ordinary appearance in order to adopt other disguises depending on the situation

---

*The *komuso* were wandering monks of the Fuke sect, a branch of Zen. Membership of this sect was restricted to failed *bushi* (warriors). For this reason they were not obliged to shave their heads and they also had the right to carry a sword. Another characteristic feature that is quite important was the fact they wore large straw hats that concealed their faces, as emphasized in this passage from the *Shoninki*.

†The *katana* is a sword with a long blade (twenty-three inches or longer), the one used most frequently by the samurai (and more specifically called then *uchi-gatana* or *daito*), while the wakizashi is a short-bladed sword or, if you rather, a large dagger (lengths varied from twelve to twenty-three inches), which was generally the ninja's preference. During the Edo Period (1600–1868), only samurai had the right to carry weapons, but civilian travelers had the right to carry wakizashis for their protection while on the road. The *yakuza* (outlaws who had banded together as a brotherhood or militia) carried the longest possible wakizashis, almost the size of the katana (uchi-gatana).

‡The majority of people in feudal Japan were peasants; this is why the seventh or "normal" disguise is frequently translated as "farmer."

Prepare yourself well by using these different disguises, based on the circumstances. It is essential to know yourself, to study the place where you are staying, and to conceal yourself there with a serene heart.

Profile-Shifting in Today's World

Today, these ancient forms of disguise are, of course, completely incompatible with modern society. This in no way invalidates the utility and effectiveness of *henso-jutso* (technique of profile-shifting). Like all ninja techniques, the capacity to adopt a disguise is timeless and can never go out of fashion. It is adaptable to all eras, even if the specific details and forms vary through the ages. Even in the time of the ninjas, this identification of seven disguises was created as a guide: a basis for improvisation rather than a restriction.

USING KNOWLEDGE OF THE FIVE PLEASANT THINGS

In the tradition of the Kishu-ryu (kishu no tsutae) it is said that there are five pleasant things:

1. *Bijo binan:* beautiful women and handsome men
2. *Denoku daishu:* sumptuous palaces and expensive residences
3. *Kansho ganshui:* calm and well-ventilated places

4. *Denraku kabu:* artistic performances and spectacles
5. *Bunpitsu gako:* arts and literature

Those who are attracted by beautiful women, handsome men, luxurious palaces, calm spaces, impressive rivers, artists, and art can also renounce them. If you learn these five things and how to best profit from them, will there be any enemy you are incapable of defeating?

No, there will not be.

TEN METHODS OF CONCEALMENT

There are ten major methods for concealing oneself and spying (*koho junin no narai*):

1. *Onsei nin:* This is the art of concealing yourself by virtue of noise, such as music or when a horse neighs loudly while chewing on its bit.
2. *Jun nin:* This is following people with natural movements without destroying anything.
3. *Museiho nin:* During troubled times it is necessary to be ready to sacrifice everything. Even in a dead-end situation likely to produce a feeling of defeat, the enemy may be blinded by pity or overwhelmed by other feelings, which will grant you the possibility of fleeing.
4. *Nyogen nin:* No matter how slender the circumstances, you should recognize the principle at once and profit from it in order to gain an advantage over the enemy.
5. *Nyoei nin:* Under no pretext allow yourself to be separated from people; stick firmly to your goal.

6. *Nyoen nin:* During the times when people are incautious or negligent, enter their houses or their hearts.
7. *Nyomu nin:* Be capable of evaluating individuals.
8. *Nyoko nin:* Examine the enemy's territory and adapt to it.
9. *Nyoka nin:* Study the enemy's deepest depths and learn the most intimate recesses of his heart. Under these circumstances, in order to not behave suspiciously, you must act naturally or in disguise.
10. *Nyoku nin:* If an adversary has discovered that he is being spied upon, all effort to defeat him will then be in vain. Consequently, it is important to leave no trace behind when spying.

These ten basic principles must be learned and are covered in the *Shoninki* from the beginning to end. They should be considered basic knowledge and the beginning of all study. Hidden within these basic principles are higher spiritual principles of a depth beyond measure. Knowledge of these principles should be revealed to no one.

2

NECESSARY KNOWLEDGE ABOUT UNKNOWN MOUNTAIN PATHS

(*SHIRANU SANRO NO NARAI*)

━━◄►━━

If a shinobi should find himself on paths he does not know in the mountains or forest and there is no one around from whom he can ask directions, he must continue on his route and smother all feelings of anxiety or doubt. Night falls quickly in the deep forests of the mountains and it is then impossible to keep moving forward. To save time, it is necessary to stop and rest.

If you come to a fork in the road, you must decide between different paths and you may begin to have doubts and anxiety. This is when you should recite an old poem. Count the number of the kanji in the poem. If it is an odd number, take the left path; an even number, take the right. This makes it possible to free yourself from doubt and determine your path.

What is necessary in order to understand this? Without bringing the unconscious into it, you must place your trust in nature and in the path leading to Heaven. In this way, a shinobi never remains still and incredible things are made possible.

Taking the right path means looking for the path used by men. Are there footprints on the ground left by sandals, or from the passage of cows or horses? What is the state of the ground trod upon by people, the state of the grass and the trees? The paths used by men are trampled and worn. No matter how large a path may be, it will start shrinking once people no longer use it. The color of the grass and the trees can also provide clues about the paths trodden by men. The grass is trampled flat on paths that are used daily and signifies that a village is close by. A person who can distinguish freshly cut plants from those that have not been cut for a long time will thereby recognize the proximity of a village. Birds and other animals clearly know the paths used by men and avoid them.

You can follow the footprints left by men or horses on snow-covered trails. You should not stare into the air or watch the falling snow. If the path is covered by so much snow that it is no longer recognizable, or you are moving forward on a path that is totally unknown, send your horse ahead as a scout, based on the old saying, "an old horse knows his way." If all traces of the path have been made completely invisible by the snow, stick your walking staff into it. If the snow has collected over ground that is hard, keep in mind that it was hardened by being walked upon; if not, it means you have gone astray from the path. During walks through snow-covered mountains, a shinobi will stick to the crests because the snow easily slides to the bottom on steep and craggy paths.

To mark a path already traveled, use the technique of the "tied grass stems," which can help you remember your trail. You can also rely on signs left beforehand, or natural landmarks, or orient yourself based on footsteps. If you realize that you are on the wrong path, find the right one as quickly as possible and follow it.

USE AND CONSTRUCTION OF THE KAIRO

When it is snowing and quite cold, use a kairo as protection against the cold. The kairo can also be used at any time for other purposes.

There are several ways to construct a kairo. First, cut slits on the sides of a tube that is five or six *suns** long and around four or five suns in diameter. A coat of arms or emblems can be placed on the base, if you desire, to allow the light to shine through. Inside place a piece of cloth dipped in water or even a piece of crumpled wool wrapped around a shaft made from a thin iron bar. Then pull out the bar and replace it with a thicker piece of pipe. Next, pour an inflammable liquid into it, along with the carbonized corpse of an animal,† and cover the entire thing in paper. Make an opening at one end to let the fire through. You can do the same with paper made from cedar bark. When the kairo has been completely wrapped up, add a mixture that will allow the fire to burn for a long period of time. You should scrupulously follow the proven instructions when using these different methods.

---

*Like the shaku, the *sun* (pronounced "soun") is another old Japanese unit of measurement; it is equivalent to 1.19 inches (or a tenth of a shaku). A kairo was therefore a cylinder measuring around six or seven inches with a diameter of five to six inches.
†The animal in question was generally an amphibious salamander. Healing properties were attributed to its body when grilled.

Methods have been developed to allow the fire to burn as long as possible. Originally, paper and other material were put in mixtures prepared from kaki fruits or eggplants and then blended with gray-yellow magnolia (*ho*), young sprouts of a bitter herb that had been aged one year (*inutade*), kaki nuts, or pieces of wooden boards. This mixture was finally placed in the kairo to carbonize. The kairo was then placed in the chest pocket. Filled with coals of the inutade, a kairo could keep a shinobi warm for an entire day.

The Kairo in Context

As indicated earlier, the kairo was a kind of portable hot water bottle. It was generally a metal cylinder holding burning hot pumice stones wrapped in cloth or a wick fed by kerosene. This contraption gave its bearer welcome warmth in the cold, especially useful for a ninja who could use it to warm his hands and fingers before undertaking an operation. This would prevent the loss of skill because of swollen fingers.

The kairo also had another function. It could be used as a light source for discreet illumination or for sending signals at night.

Use of the kairo was not widespread in Japan until 1688–1704. In the context of the *Shoninki,* written in 1681, it was a very rare and innovative technology known only to a few rare individuals. This explains why this passage from the book lingers so long on the methods for manufacturing one. It also shows how the ninja were always ahead of their time, at "the spearhead of progress"; they never hesitated to adapt their ancient traditions and methods to promptly integrate the most modern scientific innovations, contrary to the samurai, who were clearly of a more conservative, even reactionary, mentality.

3

TRAVELING BY FOOT AT NIGHT
(*YOMICHI NO KOTO*)

lthough it is easier to hide when walking at night than
during the day, you should bear in mind that people
are more suspicious during this time. Consequently, it is necessary to avoid acting in any way that is conspicuous. When
a shinobi can no longer recognize his way in the dark, he
should sit down and contemplate the heavens, observing the
stars through the clouds. This observation will allow him to
recognize his route. Also, paths that are much trodden by
men have a high salt content, which can be verified by tasting
the dirt with the tongue.

When a path runs alongside fences, it is easy to be
fooled into thinking that the fence posts are human beings.
However, on looking at them more closely, the shinobi will
see that they have been constructed in a regular manner and
that it is very difficult for men to exhibit such regularity. If
there is still any doubt as to whether an object is a shrub, a
tree, or a person, you should remember that sooner or later
a man will move. Immediately sit on the ground and calmly
observe the object for a while. If it should prove to be a per-

son, though he will try not to move a muscle, he will eventually do just that.

THE USE AND OBSERVATION OF LIGHT

Whoever catches sight of a light at night should sit down and watch the light. Light carried by someone moving away will shrink and light carried by someone coming closer will get larger. Naturally, the shinobi can always glide to the right or left.

If an experienced servant is carrying an individual light, he will walk in a straight line. If he meets any younger people on his path, he will turn his light in the direction opposite the one from which they approach. This is a strategy for walking in the shadows cast by other people. If you encounter an enemy while carrying a torch, point it at him and turn in his direction in one move, so that you can skirt him and get behind him.

If you strike a light in a darkened house, the greatest caution is required; you should in all cases never act without thinking. Lighting something in front of you means blinding yourself and being unable to see anything. A shinobi lights a flame in the shadow of his body so that light emanates from him.

When walking at night on paths illuminated by the moon, walk in the shadows. When meeting undesirable people, hide your face in your hands and disappear immediately.

THE WAYS OF WALKING

Avoid making any noises with your *zori*⋅ at night. It is tradition to not drag your feet while walking, not only because it is incorrect but also because of the noise it causes and the danger it incurs of being easily detected. However, the adversary also knows the strategy of the zori,* so the shinobi uses the "changing shoe" strategy to make different noises while walking.

Distinctions are made between different kinds of footsteps:

Nuki-ashi: stealthy step
Suri-ashi: rubbing step
Shime-ashi: tight step
Tobi-ashi: flying step
Kata-ashi: one step
O-ashi: giant step
Ko-ashi: little step
Kizami-ashi: small step
Wari-ashi: quick step
Tsuene-no-ashi: normal step

These are the ten ways of walking (*ashi nami jukka jo*).

---

*Zori are a kind of Japanese flip-flop made from straw (as opposed to *waraji*, sandals made from straw that has been woven into cords). A shinobi could change them in order to make different noises that would fool his foe, or to walk more quietly. He could also leave fake footprints behind him, using sandals with specially carved soles that could leave the desired footprints on the ground behind him: animal tracks, those of a large or small man, and so forth.

Ninjutsu's Ten Ways of Walking

The fact that the author of the *Shoninki* only draws up a simple list of these ten techniques, without supplying any detail, demonstrates the fact that this text was primarily an aide-memoire, providing the broad lines and major principles of ninjutsu, with the details then transmitted orally from teacher to student. The ten types can be further elucidated as follows:

1. *Nuki-ashi* (the stealthy step): a silent step made by lifting up the heels high, a walking technique sometimes compared to the movement of the octopus, and mainly used when walking on floorboards (to avoid making them creak)

2. *Suri-ashi* (the rubbing step): walking silently with a short sliding step

3. *Shime-ashi* (the tight step): walking silently while placing the heel down first

4. *Tobi-ashi* (the flying step): walking while making a small leap with one of the toes

5. *Kata-ashi* (one step): jumping while only using one foot

6. *O-ashi* (the giant step): walking with large strides, used mainly for walking through tall grass

7. *Ko-ashi* (the little step): walking with short strides, a kind of walk inspired by that of the heron, and mainly used for walking through shallow bodies of water

8. *Kizami-ashi* (the small step): walking with strides that are only a foot in length.

9. *Wari-ashi* (the quick step): walking with the feet pointing in opposite directions

10. *Tsuene-no-ashi* or *tsune ashi* (the normal step): walking normally

It should be also pointed out that there is a "sideways walk" (*yoko-aruki*), also known as "the crab walk" (*kani-aruki*), which is typically ninja.

4

ENTERING ENEMY HOUSES

(*KINJUKU TORI HAIRU NARAI*)

———◄►———

Despite the feeling of unease a shinobi may feel when entering houses that have already been scouted as well as entering unknown gardens adjacent to residences, not to mention those of the enemy, this kind of operation is one of his primary duties.

If someone is more or less suspicious, depending on the province or the place, the shinobi will spend a certain amount of time, on several occasions, without being noticed, to reconnoiter the premises. When an opportune moment arises, the shinobi will feign illness in front of the gate of the house he wishes to sneak into. He will lie down pretending to be too weak to move, and ask for medicine or for hot or cold water to drink.

The illnesses that you can use to your advantage this way are the stomach aches caused by worms,* sunstroke, gastric

---

*During this era, it was thought in Japan that most illness was caused by various tiny evil creatures entering the human body, as shown, notably, in the medical book *Harikikigaki,* written in 1568 (which describes no less than sixty-three of these pathogenic creatures and the means to fight them). A stomachache, known as *omushi,* was thought to be caused by large worms.

distress, a heart attack, or diarrhea. It is not advisable to pretend to be drunk. After having obtained boiling water and pretending that you feel better, you should seize this opportunity to be taken inside the house and make the acquaintance of the master of the household while presenting a respectful attitude, and then leave the house.

You should next return with a gift, expressing the deepest gratitude, and give the master of the house a letter of thanks. Once this is done, you can draw closer. If you are establishing relations with the inhabitants of a house, first choose to form bonds of friendship with the children. If you offer gifts, it is advised to do so secretly at first. Over time, you can expand to include those individuals among the functionaries you think highly of, taking pains not to make any distinction between men and women. This will certainly delight the master of the house and he may speak to the gift-giver. This is how it is possible to gather information.

There is a proverb that says:

> *Metal tends to adapt to fire*
> *Men seek to conform to what they say*
> *The nightingale's beak eats nothing in the*
>   *flower*
> *It only delights in its delicious aroma.*

ASSESSING AN AREA AND TROOPS

To learn the topographical relief of an area, the shinobi should be able to observe it from an appropriate distance and estimate it. In territory you intend to reconnoiter, you should mingle with civil servants or pass yourself off as a merchant, and remain in the same place for two or three days.

To count the number of homes in a place, you should fill both your sleeves with a certain number of beans or small stones, and drop them one by one when passing before the entrances of the houses. You can count the inhabited houses with the right sleeve and the uninhabited ones with the left sleeve. When you are finished, you can count the remaining stones, and then you will definitely know how many inhabited and uninhabited houses there are.

To count the number of individuals when soldiers march past, the same principle is applied to distinguish between foot soldiers, horsemen, or lancers. Put a number of stones or beans in your sleeves corresponding to the number in each category. In certain places, you can also determine the number of horses when on narrow roads, bridges, or alongside houses.

It is possible that under certain circumstances, it will not be possible to take a count, but this is no excuse for losing sight of your purpose. To obtain information necessary for attaining your objective, you should get into the good graces of the functionaries by feigning ignorance and by giving them gifts at the same time. Information is available in high quantity from those in subaltern positions because—though the functionaries desire to please their bosses—they receive nothing from them in return but scorn. This is the nature of hierarchical superiors.

5

THE TEACHINGS OF WOLVES AND FOXES

(*KORO NO MICHI NO NARAI*)

Foxes and wolves are very cunning animals: it is said that the fox can deceive man and that the wolf can read his very soul. They travel indirect routes and can solve the most difficult problems in an incredible manner. Although the techniques based on their example are extremely rare, it is absolutely useful to study them.

When traveling along the official roads in enemy territory, you run the risk of stumbling into a checkpoint. So under no circumstances should a shinobi ever take these roads. Instead, use the technique employed by wolves and foxes, and stay away from the main roads; take the secondary routes. You should use the routes used by the native inhabitants, which are located a distance of at least two or three *ri** from the checkpoints. You need to find a good pretext for using these roads. Depending on the situation and the desired objective,

*A *ri* is an old Japanese unit of measurement equivalent to 2.468 miles. Two or three ri would therefore be the equivalent of around 5 to 7.5 miles.

it may be necessary to disguise yourself as a priest, a mountain monk, or a merchant.

In principle it is preferable for a shinobi to travel alone. First of all, he can then go wherever he wishes. If he is disguised as an itinerant monk, he can also be accompanied by two or three other shinobi. One of them should be an expert in languages (*dakko no shinobi*), capable of speaking the different dialects of sixty regions as well as capable of taking note of the important areas and places visited.

The person who acts out of duress has lost the favor of heaven. The techniques of these kinds of experts are not handed down to their descendants. As quickly as pigeon eggs are speedily discovered, they become victims.

You should keep this in mind and ponder on it.

6

THE TEACHINGS
OF OXEN AND HORSES
(*GYUBA NO TSUTAE NO KOTO*)

◄─►

This strategy is the opposite of that of wolves and foxes because cattle and horses move about openly among men. If a general wishes to send messengers into enemy territory, he chooses shinobi who can pass as members of the common people and thus can reach the intended territory.

Another possibility lies in the fact that a shinobi can meet a messenger from the targeted province at a set time, and then have that individual accompany him into enemy territory. This corresponds exactly to the way cows and horses are led by their masters, and this is the reason the strategy was given this name.

To devote yourself to gathering information, it is sometimes necessary, depending on the circumstances, to reside in the land of the adversary. The shinobi will be given complete latitude for thinking up a good reason for this: he can form bonds of friendship with people, pretend to be ill, marry a woman, speak ill of his own land and even laud the enemy country, and thereby pass for a traitor to his own country.

7

GATHERING INFORMATION IN TEMPLES AND SANCTUARIES

(GUJI KEIMON NO NARAI)

————◄ ►————

To learn about certain territories, you can visit their temples and sanctuaries,* and generously distribute money and gifts while there.

If you introduce yourself simply as an individual, this may arouse some suspicion, but if you present yourself as a priest or villager, these doubts will be dispelled. If you give out money, you can help yourself, and if, moreover, you are invited to dine, you can ask the questions you want in return for a glass of alcohol. If there is word that plots are being hatched in the province, you can also learn about them from the prayers and sermons in the temples and sanctuaries. If you discuss plots

---

*During the Tokugawa Era (1602–1868), members of the Japanese clergy were charged by the government to perform administrative duties in addition to their religious ones, particularly that of keeping written records with information about the families and various individuals who were members of their temples. This is similar to Western clergy being made responsible for keeping parish registers by royal authority. These written records were a gold mine of information about the region's inhabitants for any ninja who could manage to consult them in return for a bribe to the priest.

with the high priest and he boasts of the incredible power and distinctions of the gods, you can continue loosening his tongue with alms.

This is the principle on which is based the gathering of information in temples and sanctuaries; consequently you should establish your plans accordingly.

To obtain information about the provinces, it is also possible to visit brothels, bathhouses, amusement quarters, or gaming houses.

8

DISCUSSION ON CHANGES IN APPEARANCE

(*HENGE NO RON*)

———◄ ►———

People say that *kitsune* (foxes) and *tanuki* (raccoon dogs) change shape to deceive the eyes of men and even that they live among them. We humans are not given the ability to change our shape. If you skillfully use a disguise, it is necessary to stay on your guard to keep deceiving people while they can see you. Even if a large number of subterfuges, which should work well, have been passed on to us, it is very important to remain vigilant and on your guard. A person who disguises himself without conviction and without altering his appearance sufficiently will be quickly unmasked. This is a technique that must be studied in depth and very seriously.

Kitsune and *Tanuki:* The Two Most Popular Characters of the Fantasy Bestiary of Japanese Folklore

Kitsune refers to the fox. The *tanuki* is the raccoon dog, a member of the fox family that looks like a raccoon. This animal has the distinct feature of being the sole canine in the world that hibernates. It is frequently mistaken for a badger or a raccoon.

The tanuki is rather a buffoon-type figure. He appears in countless children's songs, and it is not rare that he is depicted with enormous, even disproportionately large testicles. A drunkard and a glutton, folklore gives him the ability to take human shape and temporarily transform dead leaves into banknotes. This allows him to buy large quantities of saké from human merchants, who become distraught when the banknotes turn back into dead leaves. Meanwhile the tanuki gets drunk on their wine while relishing the fine trick he has pulled.

Less favorable than the tanuki, but not necessarily evil, the kitsune also possesses the ability to transform to look like a human. He also possesses a wider variety of much stronger magic powers, which increase with age. Japanese folklore maintains that as the fox grows older his powers are enhanced and he grows additional tails. The most powerful kitsune have nine tails! The kitsune can take possession of human beings or drive them mad, breathe fire or ignite a blaze by rubbing his tails together, create illusions, curve time and space, and so on.

Several elements of the ninja tradition make reference to these two animals. For example, in the evasion techniques used for hiding and disappearing, two techniques prompt ninja to imitate these two creatures. First is *tanuki-gakure-no-jutsu:* this means to climb trees in which to hide as the tanuki does, mainly by pressing up closely against the trunk so that you and the tree appear as one. The second is *kitsune-gakure-no-jutsu:* this means to hide under the water like the fox does to conceal itself.

The *Banshenshukai* (vol. 6) also mentions a technique the ninja sometimes used to move around when infiltrating enemy houses, the name of which refers to this animal—the "fox walk" (*kitsune ashi, kitsune bashiri,* or *kitsune aruke*). This is a rapid form of walking in a zig-zag while staying low to the ground, with the body pulled tightly together to form as small a target as possible. To do this, the ninja walks on the tips of his fingers and toes (somewhat like a sprinter on the starting blocks at the start of a race).

We should also note that the powers traditionally attributed to the "fox spirits" (changing appearance, illusions, invisibility, pyrotechnics, and so on) are the same ones with which the nijna are customarily credited. This underscores the natural and mystical origins of ninjutsu.

On a mission, you should wear a long *ama-baori,* a cape, or something similar in order to change your appearance. The eyebrows should be redrawn on the face, the teeth coated with a metallic color, the chin altered, the face darkened, and the hair tousled. You can also wear a beard.

The secret of a successful disguise with painting depends on the combination of colors and immediate appearance. You should avoid unsuitable blends. There are three different color blends that can be used to stain your face: light-colored ink is blended with red cinnabar; light white is blended with small es of cork, cinnabar, or yellow-earth; and indigo or crimson is added to ink that is the color of cork.

The term "fake illness" (*kyobyo*) is used to designate pretending to be an invalid. When doing this you should not sleep, use *moxa*,* let your hair grow, and refrain from cutting your fingernails or toenails or bathing. You should wear unkempt clothing and a headband.

As the number of moments and situations that will confront you are so many and varied, it is important to be adaptable.

---

*Moxa comes from the Japanese word *mogusa,* which in turn comes from the expression *mo kusa,* meaning "herb that one burns." Its basic ingredient is dried, crushed mugwort. Moxa is used in moxibustion, a therapeutic method of Chinese origin based on the same principles as acupuncture. But instead of thin needles, moxa that has been formed into small cones or balls is used to heat or slightly burn the acupuncture points.

9

INFILTRATING ARMED TROOPS

(JINCHU SHINOBU TOKI NO NARAI)

The technique of infiltrating armies is very important. When attempting to infiltrate, you should prepare for the possibility of beating a retreat at any moment. Before an attempt is made to infiltrate armies on a battlefield, the enemy's attention must be diverted with the use of some "wolf fire"* shot by the allied side. If this is not a possibility, you should attempt to infiltrate at the very moment the troops are starting to march, cutting down wood and bamboo, raising camp, or falling asleep after the exertions of the day, or you should use the shield provided by a heavy rain or violent wind. An old tradition also says that you should know and easily master the way the enemy soldiers stand and sit down, as well as their signs, passwords, and methods of saluting.

The technique of blending in with the local populace should be attempted only with people who are solidly established and

---

*This term describes bursts of light similar to fireworks that were used by commanders to transmit orders to their troops.

in no case around *bushi,** people who inspire fear. If you run into people who are talking about this thing or that, you should also talk and know what they are talking about.

If you are discovered, the sentinels will shout, which can be used to divert attention on to other people and you can take advantage of the noise to hide. You should not be tied to any particular spot and everything should be considered as a potential hiding place. If it is almost impossible for a shinobi to find a hiding spot, he should trust his fate to Heaven and walk forward fearlessly. Likely spots for hiding are old springs, shadows, mountaintops, holes and caves, toilets, large trees, the scaffolding of buildings under construction, and in public places where you would not be expected to hide. Places where it is easy to hide will be considered suspect by the enemy and they should consequently be avoided.

---

*The word *bushi* designates the entire Japanese caste of warriors and soldiers (of which the samurai are only a part). Exercising the right of life and death over commoners as their whims took them, the bushi were often envied but not necessarily esteemed. During times of war, they would sometimes indulge themselves in certain abuses common to soldiers on a military campaign. Because they inspired a certain amount of mistrust and wariness, ninja were advised not to disguise themselves as soldiers.

10

MEDITATIONS ON WATER BIRDS

(*MIZUDORI NO KANGAE*)

————◄►————

Let's consider we are looking at a place where enemy spies are present as well as our own.* Even if it makes his heart race nervously, the shinobi should approach matters serenely like a water bird. The men of this world allow themselves to be so easily distracted by many things while a shinobi permits nothing to turn him from the path he follows to his goal, containing within himself both confidence and sincerity. This path is the same that is trod by a bodhisattva or a person striving to attain illumination.

> *The Shishui River of Hunan*
> *Blue as the sky.*

———————

*This point indicates that the author of the *Shoninki* was not only writing a treatise from the perspective of sending ninja to attack an enemy but also had defense in mind, foreseeing that the enemy could also have recourse to these kinds of agents and identical techniques. It is a way of reminding the reader that a crucial precept of the "art of war" is that of always looking at things with two points of view. A good strategy of attack is only half effective if it does not also include a good defense strategy.

In the middle a water bird white as snow,
I aspire to become like him.

Water birds and other wild animals are often seen around castles and their moats, stone walls, and other hard-to-reach places where spies will surely take up position. If a noise is heard, it is most often birds taking off in flight.[*]

During the times that spies conceal themselves around castles, the birds fly off, the sky becomes cloudy, and the light of the stars wanes. Spying means blending in with the widest variety of things and, in this way, concealing yourself skillfully and with art.

To cross a body of water, construct a rectangular assemblage out of wood or bamboo, made from four pieces of wood tied together. If you hide in the water, you should choose a spot by the trunk of a large tree that will allow you to lift your head from the water. To breathe while under the water, a shinobi uses either a bamboo tube or the *saya* of his wakizashi.[†]

---

[*]If water birds suddenly erupt in flight, it is most likely because a foreign presence or an unfamiliar noise scared them. This provides good grounds for suspecting the presence of a ninja or enemy agent in the area.

[†]*Saya* is the word for the rigid scabbard that houses the blade of a Japanese sword, whether it is short (like the wakizashi) or long (like the katana). By piercing the tip and using the other end as a mouthpiece, the ninja could use his saya to breathe while underwater. Incidentally, if a bamboo tube was used, this, too, could serve as a weapon, namely a blowgun. The techniques mentioned in this chapter come from *suiren-jutsu* (mastering the aquatic element, for silent swimming or fighting in it) and *suiton-jutsu* (using water to hide and disappear).

Someone wishing to scale the battlements should either use a kaginawa or the rope used to tie the boards of the water craft together. Elongated objects, resembling the *kogai*,* can be inserted inside the crevices of the castle's stone wall.

Kogai were a pair of long wooden or metal pins carried by samurai. They had multiple uses. Originally they were used to scratch the head when wearing a helmet. The kogai then transformed into multipurpose tools: hairpins, curry combs for horses, and so on. It is easy to see how such objects would quickly reveal their value to ninjas for scaling walls, by being used as rods planted in the cracks of the stones forming ramparts or battlements.

11

THE OPPORTUNE MOMENTS FOR INFILTRATION

(*SHINOBI HAIRU JIBUN NO KOTO*)

It is standard practice not to set a time to begin an infiltration but to use the opportune moment when people are occupied or have dropped their guard. It is important to proceed without haste and to precisely determine the objective to be achieved.

Normally, people go to bed around nine or ten o'clock, falling asleep after about two hours, and wake up around six o'clock in the morning, but this varies depending on the individual. There are people who breathe very irregularly when asleep and other who breathe regularly. Others keep their eyes open even for an hour or so after falling asleep. Then there are those people who drop off to sleep all at once, like a roof caving in.

The best times for sneaking in are:

At night: at dusk, at the hour of the Boar, the hour of the Rat, the hour of the Ox, and the hour of the Tiger.

During the day: at the hour of the Hare, and the hour of the Rooster.*

Time and the Twelve Animals

In feudal Japan, the time and the directions were designated by the name of the twelve animals of traditional astrology. The Japanese hour was close to two of our current hours, its actual duration varying slightly depending on the season.

Hour of the Rat (*ne*): from 11:00 PM to 1:00 AM

Hour of the Ox (*ushi*): 1:00 AM to 3:00 AM

Hour of the Tiger (*tora*): 3:00 AM to 5:00 AM

Hour of the Hare (*u*): 5:00 AM to 7:00 AM

Hour of the Dragon (*tatsu*): 7:00 AM to 9:00 AM

Hour of the Serpent (*mi*): 9:00 AM to 11:00 AM

Hour of the Horse (*uma*): 11:00 AM to 1:00 PM

Hour of the Sheep (*hitsuji*): 1:00 PM to 3:00 PM

Hour of the Ape (*saru*): 3:00 PM to 5:00 PM

Hour of the Rooster (*tori*): 5:00 PM to 7:00 PM

Hour of the Dog (*inu*): 7:00 PM to 9:00 PM

Hour of the Boar (*inoshishi*): 9:00 PM to 11:00 PM

---

*To simplify matters, the most propitious hours for infiltration were between five and seven o'clock in the evening and between nine o'clock at night and seven o'clock in the morning.

If you do not know the best time, you should let your body resolve the matter. If the left side of your nose is insensitive, you should choose an even hour, and if it is the right side, you should choose an odd hour. This behavior is like the pupils of the cat's eyes, which expand or shrink without people really knowing why.*

Telling Time by the Pupils of a Cat's Eyes

Having no watches, but always astute and keen observers of nature, the ninja perfected a technique for telling the time by careful examination of a cat's eyes: *nekome-jutsu.* This is often translated by the amusing term, the "cat-clock technique."

Daylight generally varies in a regular fashion in accordance with the course of the sun, and the eyes of cats also vary just as regularly in tune with that rhythm. Their pupils grow large during the early morning and evening in order to capture the maximum amount of light when it is at its weakest, and shrink to their smallest point at noon, when the sunlight is at its peak. This is how the ninja were able to establish the following schema for telling the time by looking at the eyes of cats.

• During the earliest hours of the day, while it was still

*This passage should not be taken literally. It basically means that you should trust in your own experience and especially your inner feelings at the time to determine the precise moment for action. An intuition that has emerged from your depths while you are in harmony with your environment is *just like that displayed by the pupils of the cat, which naturally change in tune with external conditions.*

dark, the cat's pupils were dilated to their maximum extent, completely round and in the form of a "ball."

- As the sun rose and the light increased, the cat's pupils would then shrink until they became as small as possible around noon, when they took on the shape of "needles."
- In between they went through the stage of the "egg" and the "seed" as they shrank.
- Then, as the light began waning in the afternoon, the cat's pupils would begin to enlarge and go back through the previous stages in the opposite direction: "seed," "egg," and "ball."

In the early morning you should carry several small stones with you. Move very cautiously; if you are tired, it is necessary to take some other things. If you are climbing onto a roof or along a wall, you should help yourself, as mentioned earlier, with a kaginawa, katana, or wakizashi. Scaling a roof and walking upon it should be done in silence, while being mindful of its ridge and two slopes. If something appears that seems bizarre to the eyes of the shinobi, he should toss a stone in that direction and watch the reaction.

The shinobi who has been discovered should cast a stone on the ground while fleeing, making a clear and loud sound. This ruse will allow him to get away.*

---

*This passage alludes to the technique called *yogijakure-jutsu*. It consists of causing a diversion by tossing a small pebble or any other little object (preferably metallic, such as a coin) to make a noise in another direction to temporarily distract the attention of a pursuer or a sentinel on guard.

12

THE TEACHINGS
OF THE QUADRUPEDS
(*YO ASHAI NO NARAI*)

━━◄ ►━━

This is the technique that consists of imitating four-legged animals like dogs and cats. With the help of this knowledge, a shinobi can hide in the darkness of the night or in places where it will be hard to spot him. The implication of imitating the quadrupeds consists not only of taking their shape but also of behaving like them.*

To learn something about dogs, first observe the habit they have of digging holes at the foot of fences or walls.†

---

*According to the *Banshenshukai* (vol. 6), there are several movement techniques for infiltrating enemy houses, among them the "dog walk" (*inu bashiri* or *inu aruki*). This is a variant of the "fox walk," but in the "dog walk" the hands and feet are placed flat on the ground. Like the "fox walk," the "dog walk" is used to move while in a low position, or because the place the ninja must move through is not very high.

†By looking for holes at the bottom of a fence, the ninja can determine whether he can expect to find a dog in the house he has targeted. This habit of dogs can also inspire the ninja to dig out a small depression in the ground that will allow him to slip beneath a wall or fence by crawling in order to enter an enemy house discreetly.

While they are digging, dogs give a signal by emitting a low growl or by whimpers. They do the same while sleeping, lying down, or shaking themselves. They can emit a similar sound when tugging on the bottom of a pair of pants. If dogs encounter a wild animal, they customarily growl. In contrast, they bark when threatening a human being. When a dog is in the street, he hugs the fences and the walls. When he rests on the ground, he does so in the shade during the summer and in the sunlight during the winter. If a dog barks aggressively at people, it is undoubtedly a mean dog.

Whoever wants to earn the good graces of a dog should give him some cooked food to eat. If you add some sesame seeds and fritters, he will stop barking. If the dog is given *machin** to eat, he will become intoxicated immediately and become as if dead. Then, if water is sprinkled on him, the dog will come back to his senses. His death is a certainty if iron filings are introduced into his food. Because dogs have the habit of barking at people, the shinobi does not like them and he must keep an eye on their reactions.

It is even easier to imitate a cat than a dog. This will not be treated in detail here as there are many people capable of imitating cats without any problem.

Machin is the name for a typical tree of Southeast Asia, the strychnine tree (*Strychnos nux-vomica*). Strychnine, a poison that paralyzes the nervous system, is made from the seeds inside the fruits of this tree. Depending on its preparation, the same substance can be used for medicinal purposes or for rat poison.

13

THE TASK OF TWO SHINOBI WORKING TOGETHER

(*FUTARI SHINOBI NO KOTO*)

———◄ ►———

It is much more difficult for two people to spy together than it is for one alone. Two shinobi should be able to merge together as one single person so as to avoid any doubt on how an operation will be carried out. If they are not in agreement and cannot find harmony, even if only about the smallest thing, one of the two will override the other one.

When, for example, two people are spying at night, one of them knocks at the gate or main door to lure people out, and then runs away. This seems suspicious to the inhabitants of the house and they will chase him. This is the time the second one can use to get into the house. Or one of the two shinobi can pretend to be a messenger and ask to see the master of the house to give him a false letter. At the same time the second shinobi can stealthily enter the dwelling. Another possibility is to quarrel violently and noisily. When one of the two shinobi flees into the house, the other pursues him. If the fleeing person is invited to stay by the head of the household, he can take advantage of it to gather information about the house and to open locks and doors.

These are several simple examples that can vary and also suggest other procedures, inspiring and enriching other ideas, which is of capital importance.

14

THE TASK OF THREE SHINOBI WORKING TOGETHER

(*SANNIN SHINOBI NO KOTO*)

I n the case of three individuals working together, the same problems appear as with two individuals. If there are more than three people, the method still remains the same. When hearts are beating as one, great things can be achieved using this method. But it can be problematic when not all the shinobi have received the same training, because one who is not as experienced can become a stumbling block for the others. Cases like this have made work difficult even in the past. In comparison, the work of a shinobi alone is much easier.

But when three people have an understanding, it is possible to infiltrate any place. For example, steep places or castle moats can be investigated and conquered: two shinobi lend their shoulders to the third and make his ascent possible. He can then pull the others up.

As a diversion one shinobi can grab a young man and shout: "Stop, thief!" When it has been established that he is no thief and the attention of other passersby has been captured, then you can offer him excuses. A shinobi can take advantage of the uproar this causes to take to his heels. As has been explained earlier, with three individuals, a brawl can be simulated between two people. Under cover of the confusion, the third can quietly enter the place of his choosing. Another possibility would be for one of the three to disguise himself as an official functionary who has arrested two individuals and enters a house to inspect it and inventory its contents.

With attention to detail and creative ideas, there is nothing that three people cannot undertake and carry through to the end.

If the number of participants has to be increased, then the use of passwords and a secret language will be essential.

PART THREE

Shoninki Chukan

MIDDLE SCROLL
OF THE *SHONINKI*

1

THE DOCTRINE OF THE COURSE OF EARTH AND HEAVEN

(*TENDO CHIDO NO NARAI*)

*T*endo chido* is the art of diversion, such as making something suspicious appear in the sky to divert people's attention upward while at the same time doing something on the ground that appears negligible. This strategy needs to be clearly understood. If, for example, you have the intention of hiding in a ditch or digging a passage underneath an earthen wall, you can create a diversion in a higher location. If you have to climb something, you can draw people's attention to the ditch.

But such methods do not exhaust all the possibilities of the *tendo* technique. Those using it should also pay attention to the conditions of the weather (*tenchi*). Even in favorable circumstances, such as when, among other things, the wind is blowing, it is raining, or the sun or moon is shining, if you feel uneasy within, then you should not spy. Consequently, it is deceptive to predetermine certain moments for action as being very favorable for information-gathering. If a shinobi is exhausted or indecisive, he should not undertake any action. Although a rainy night is favorable for espionage, the conditions can become dangerous depending on the place and the moment.

An expert can recognize times like these and will not undertake anything, because he takes his personal feelings into account. It is extremely difficult to read and comprehend this correctly. Let's consider a person who is capable of recognizing a propitious moment. So what did he do before this time? He used the technique for dissipating the fog and giving ease to the heart. He looked at the stars and other indications.

Stars of the Four Quarters:
Ki, Heki, Yoku, and *Shin*

In the traditional Chinese astronomical system, a cycle equivalent to the twenty-eight-day lunar month is divided into fourths, each represented as an animal and a direction:

First Quarter: the green dragon of the East
Second Quarter: the black tortoise of the North
Third Quarter: the white tiger of the West
Fourth Quarter: the red phoenix of the South

Each quarter contains seven "lunar lodges." Each of these twenty-eight "lunar lodges" was represented by a star of fixed reference, itself referring to a specific Chinese constellation. Similarly, each "lodge" also corresponded to a day in the lunar month, which was astrologically charged with good or bad fortune for certain activities.

Ki Stars

The *Ki* stars (or *Ji-Xiu* 箕 宿 ; *Mi-boshi* in Japanese) belong to the first quarter (the green dragon of the East). They designate the former Chinese constellation of the Basket. It consisted of four stars that partially correspond to our constellation Sagittarius. Its reference star corresponds to our star γ *Sagittarii*. This reference star also designates the seventh day of the lunar month, the last day of the first quarter.

Astrologically speaking, this was a good time to work the land, dig out a place for a pond or other body of water, increase stocks, collect money, or alter a construction. It was an inauspicious day for marriages and funerals.

Heki Stars

The *Heki* stars (or Donghi-Xiu 壁 宿 ; *Namame-boshi* in Japanese) belong to the second quarter (the black tortoise of the North). They designate the old Chinese constellation of the Wall, which consisted of two stars. It corresponds primarily with our constellation Pegasus (but is also a slight portion of the horse in Andromeda). Its reference star corresponds with our star γ *Pegasi*. It also designates the fourteenth day of the lunar month, the last day of the second quarter.

Astrologically, this was a good day to open a business, travel, get married, make clothes, and start new undertakings.

Yoku Stars

The *Yoku* stars (or *Yi-Xiu* 翼 宿; *Tasuki-boshi* in Japanese) belong to the third quarter (the white tiger of the West). They designate the old Chinese constellation of the Wings. This constellation is made up of twenty-two stars that primarily correspond to our constellation of the Crater in the Southern Hemisphere (with a small portion of Hydra). Its reference star corresponds with our star Alpha Crateris. It also designates the twenty-first day of the lunar month, the last day of the third quarter.

Astrologically, this was a good day to begin harvesting, changing flower beds or vegetable patches, and sowing; it was a bad day for getting married.

Shin Stars

The *Shin* stars (or *Zhen-Xiu* 軫 宿; *Mitsukake-boshi* in Japanese) belong to the fourth quarter (the red phoenix of the South). They designate the old Chinese constellation of the Chariot. This constellation consists of four stars that partially correspond with the modern constellation of Corvus. Its reference star corresponds with our star γ *Corvi*. It also designates the twenty-eighth day of the lunar month, the last day of the fourth quarter.

Astrologically, this is a good day for religious ceremonies and a poor day for making clothing.

When the four configurations of the stars, *Ki, Heki, Yoku,* and *Shin,* are traveling around the moon, there will surely be much wind. The wind is rising when the light of the lantern makes noise, and it will rain soon when the black smoke inside the lantern increases. At dawn, when the sun and moon have a halo, one can anticipate rain in three days. At dusk, the weather improves. As there are countless other methods, we shall leave this subject here.

2

ATTAINING ELEVATED AREAS
AND THE DEPTHS

(TAKA KOE HIKIKI NI HAIRU NO NARAI)

————▶——

There are differences between the various tools that a shinobi might carry with him. Some can be transported without any problem, whereas others—tools with hooks and ropes, and other, similar objects—will immediately arouse people's suspicions. For this reason, it is not advantageous to carry such tools on your person. Also, in times of emergency, for reasons of haste and rashness, a shinobi sometimes has to leave tools behind him that may be found by a third party.

You must be vigilant on this point and use the objects of everyday life for your tools. You can scale high places thanks to a kaginawa, for example. The kaginawa is made up of bamboo tubes. One *zeni** piece is placed between each tube, and a rope is inserted through them. When the rope is pulled, the

———

*A *zeni* is an ancient Japanese coin, similar to the current five-yen piece, with a hole in the middle.

kaginawa is transformed into a pole* that can be used to get over the wall.

Descending a wall is given the name *horiori*. When coming back down to the ground from a roof, the shinobi can employ a bamboo pole or a spear, by sliding down its length with his back against the wall. Furthermore, there is no excessive danger in jumping while using a long pole. When leaping with the aid of something like this, it is possible for it to slide away and one might take a nasty fall, but it will only cause minor wounds.

It is also possible, as already mentioned, to use either a long or a short sword for scaling high-perched places. However, if you do not tie the strap (*sageo*) to your leg, it will be impossible for you to regain your sword after using it this way.[†] Be extremely vigilant on this point.

---

*This implement was a grapple on the rope of which several sections of bamboo were threaded. When necessary, the ninja could pull on the rope, which would compress the pieces of bamboo against one another to their maximum extent. When locked into this position, the grapple became a solid pole, which could also serve as a weapon. Conversely, the ninja could carry this object in its tightly compact form, by pretending it was a cane or staff, then when the moment arrived, deploy it in its slackened form for use as a grapple. In this telescopic shape, the grapple was known as the *shinobikagi* or *shinobi-kurmade*.

†The *sageo* is the strap, of varying lengths, customarily used to attach a sword to the belt. When he used his sword to help him climb, the ninja firmly attached one end of the sageo to his leg. This way, he was certain not to lose his sword if he dropped it, and he was also able to pull it back out after sticking it in a crevice of the wall, so he could use it again to go higher. Climbing consisted of using the sword to ascend stage by stage. In the case of a fairly short wall, the ninja could use his sword like a step by wedging it at an angle against it, then using the sword guard (*tsuba*) for support to make it easier to jump that high. Here again, it was imperative for the ninja to have his sword tied to him in one way or another so that he could reclaim it using the sageo after he had mounted the wall.

Gird yourself with a rope when descending from high places. If you do not have any rope, firmly attach yourself with clothes that have been tied together and jump with what is left. By this means you can leap from the third floor of a place with a rope that is only two stories long, and then jump from what is the equivalent of only one story. Thanks to methods like this, you will be able to get down from any height, no matter how high it may be.

When you seek to covertly enter a building, avoid using a window that serves to let the light in, as infiltration will be made difficult by the fact that it has an inside lock. A window that is closed every day does not have such a drawback, because it has no inside lock and all you need to do is open its upper latch. Consequently, it is much easier to open.

There is a tool that is nicknamed the "central dividing strip breaker" and is used to break through earthen walls. This is a tool with a round blade of one shaku and five to six sun, similar to a toothed saw.* By pulling and turning on this implement, it is possible to effectively cut into a wall and create an opening in it. If you are trying to get through a wall or fencing, you should saw off the bottom of a barrel. Then push the barrel through the wall or fence, and crawl through the cylinder that has been made this way. When you are leaving the premises, this entrance can be closed by removing the barrel. In this way, if you are pursued, your trail can be erased as you flee and tracking you will be made more difficult for your pursuers, who will no longer be able to get through the barrier or wall.

---

*This instrument was like a round saw (*shikoro* or *noko*) around fourteen to fifteen inches in diameter.

Small saws can be adapted to unbolt doors, sliding doors, and other systems for closing rooms. To open a padlock or latch, a hole can be made through which you can insert your hand. This way you will be able to open the latch holding a door shut. Although there are a large variety of ways to keep a door shut, the lock should always be at the center or base of the door.

Now, if you want to know how an enemy spy may be attempting to get into your personal living quarters,* you must pay extremely close attention and all the doors should be locked except for one, which can be easily opened. Place a catch at the center of the door, or attach a thread to it that is connected to your pillow or your own hair; this way you may sleep tranquilly. If someone starts opening the door, it will tug on your hair.

Of course, inexperienced people will not sleep because of their lack of confidence and will remain on their guard. They will be able to tolerate this situation for two or three nights, during which time no one will be able to get in. But they will then be exhausted and fall into such a deep slumber when they do go to sleep that they will no longer be able to open their eyes when someone enters their home surreptitiously. For this reason, it is preferable to allow your body to get the appropriate amount of rest required so that it is not exhausted.

Formerly, a shinobi who sought to covertly enter a room would make a doll and throw it into the chamber, in the

---

*This is another element that indicates that the purpose of the *Shoninki* was not solely to teach its readers how to operate as ninja and conduct espionage operations, but also so they would personally know how to protect themselves and effectively counter such techniques.

expectation of some reaction. Although this is a very interesting technique, we no longer use it today.* Not everyone knows it now, but at one time it was common knowledge, and it could possibly become so again; that it is why it is wise not to use it.

---

*However, the ninja did not scorn the use of mannequins or scarecrows as a means of deceiving their adversaries about their actual location. This technique was called *ametori-jutsu*.

3

ENLARGING YOUR VIEW ANGLE DURING ESPIONAGE

(*SHINOBI NI IRO O KAERU TO IU NARAI*)

⊷►⊷

This is an important strategy when people are suspicious of being spied upon. A shinobi tries to seize upon someone in whom he can arouse temptation by virtue of something capable of evoking his enthusiasm. He can then ask anything of that person. He can pretend to be focusing on the north while he is actually spying in the south, or he can have information about faraway events transmitted to his adversary while he is actually hatching plots against that individual right at his back door.

The Master tells the talented pupil: "Steal a pitcher for me, even if it is hard to enter houses during the middle of the day to do it." The Master then also leaves; when he returns, it turns out he has bought the object he wanted. His disciple mocks him for that purchase, to which the Master responds: "You reason like a novice. If you want to acquire a large pitcher and you think of nothing else, you will not see anything but this pitcher. I, on the other hand, bow to circumstance. I stole a lot of small things that I hid up my sleeve. After I had sold them, I bought myself a large pitcher. This is what we call the strategy of enlarging one's angle of view."

To learn if someone has money, you need to develop several suitable strategies of the nature of the following technique: if someone offers to sell something that costs ten *ryo** for a cost of two or three ryo, everyone will want a piece of the action. This will leave a bitter taste in the mouths of those who have no money. Those who have no problem getting money will say that they would gladly take part in the transaction right away, if they had the money right then. By following them with a light heart and reading what's in their heart, you will be able to easily distinguish between a beggar and a rich man.

It may arise that a shinobi wishes to own something. If someone then offers him what he desires, he will keep his true intentions secret with the greatest care while negotiating the price.

To collect information about the number of people in a household or about other things, you should gain the trust of an *ana ushi*† inside the house, who will deliver the

---

*In feudal Japan, the *ryo* (or *koban*) was a gold piece. This was the common coin that held the highest value. The yen replaced it in November 1870.

†This term designates a kanji composed of the ideograms *ana* (hole) and *ushi* (cow) written one above the other. The allusion to the cow here connects it with the strategy of "oxen and horses," in which a person is sent to settle in enemy territory, so that he can invite the ninja there when the opportune moment arrives. By winning the confidence of someone inside the house, the ninja applies this "oxen strategy" to learn about a domain or a family, thanks to this individual, who is the *ana ushi*.

desired information. Recall the strategy discussed earlier that involved attracting the good graces of the master of the house. Here a shinobi should show proof of a modest heart.

4

PROTECTING YOURSELF
AGAINST THE ENEMY
(*TEKU FUSEGI TO IU NARAI*)

————◄►————

In ninjutsu you stake your life to realize your true intentions and achieve the objectives you have set. If the shinobi modestly stays in the background, he is even better positioned to spy effectively.

If the enemy is possessed by rage and in someone's debt, it is important to shift his attention onto a third party and quickly flee. Shifting your own transgression onto someone else is regarded as a sordid deed; however, these kinds of scruples have no place in the world of espionage.

Once the adversary has been infiltrated, one of the shinobi's duties is to damage the blades of his swords and break his spears.

It is easy to exploit people's rash behavior and surreptitiously sneak in when alcohol is a factor during festivals, or in the presence of prostitutes, or during games of chance involving money. Of course, the shinobi should never personally take part in these pleasures.

5

SECRET TEACHINGS FOR SOWING DISMAY IN ASSASSINS

(DAININ NI NERAWAREZARU MITSHUHO NO MAMORI)

——◄─►——

These are the most important secret teachings. The following signs should be placed in corners, in the direction of the north and south.*

As a preventive protective measure, you should always have these on your person, ritually wash yourself, ceaselessly improve yourself, and be forever on your guard.

In order to stay at people's homes freely or to protect yourself against harm, the following signs are used. If you approach the adversary, these are the magic spells that prevent you from being defeated. They will freeze people's blood and cause them to make mistakes.

A shinobi who diligently practices the rules will be able to walk over sword blades

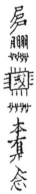

---

*As noted in the introduction, the five spells shown here arose from the Chinese principle of the five elements.

Joryakuho	Churyakuho	Geryakuho

and protect his body from wounds. He will be fearless and all arrows aimed at him will miss their target. Although a large number of magic spells exist, they are unknown to common mortals.* There are people, like women and children, who find pleasure in letting themselves be fooled by false priests and yamabushi. There is no value to this and it does not correspond with noble principles. The use of magic spells shown here also has its zone of shadow and should not be showered with exaggerated praise. Be careful when thinking about using it. Although warriors also wear magic spells on their helmets,

---

*See introduction, pages 19–20.

not all arrows miss their mark. And it is said that a person can be quickly slain by a projectile.

To disrupt people's eyesight, a shinobi will throw a product manufactured with carbonized frog eggs* in their faces or up in the air. When sneaking into houses, he can also cast it into the eyes of sleepers. When they awaken, they will be momentarily blinded.

Extreme prudence is required to avoid swallowing poison provided by other individuals. Accepting nothing to drink or eat is an important precept. Even if you are traveling in the company of someone with whom you get along well, you should still not accept any food from him. Furthermore, it is possible for poison to be slipped into rice wine, sweets, or into a bath. There was once a time when poison could be found in the food served at inns. This is why we have been handed down countless recipes for adding poisons to foods or drinks.

We use the method called "making a temporary friend" when distrust is brewing inside an infiltrated house. In this case, we must point out the necessity of talking with children, women, and men who are well-established in the house in such a way that a relationship is established with the parents or grandparents of the family, whom you do not yet know. Without realizing that they are being manipulated, their hearts will open and you can extract trustworthy information from them in just a very short time.

---

*This passage alludes to *metsubishi,* a blinding powder the ninja cast into the faces of their adversaries, either as a diversion and a means of covering their escape, or for gaining an advantage during combat. When this was not available, the ninja would use a handful of dirt, sand, ashes, or pepper. Along the same order of ideas, ninja knew how to manufacture and use smoke grenades to cover their disappearance.

6

WISELY USING THE SHADOWS CAST BY TREES

(*KIKAGE NO DAIJI*)

If you are discovered, you have no one but yourself to blame: a master of camouflage should be aware of this and find a place where he can conceal himself comfortably. If he should be discovered, it is worth the trouble to sow some doubts, which can be an anxiety-producing task.

Isn't it surprising that you can spend the entire night in the shadow of a tree? Brothels or the houses of artists are also appropriate places for spending the night and gathering information. The services of madams are favorable for any shinobi who seeks hiding, or for any man who is able to dissemble easily. Of course, with these kinds of people, the shinobi is permitted to circulate openly among them and gather information.

But at the same time he should—when speaking with the most diverse kinds of people and when able to carry on his spying activities in the best conditions—be wary of women! He should never forget this, on pain of laying himself open to the most uncomfortable situations.

7

LEAVING A TRAIL
OF FALSE CLUES BEHIND
(*KOTO O MAGIRAKASU NO NARAI*)

————◄ ►————

W hen the shinobi has been discovered and the hour of his fate has tolled, he may have failed for numerous reasons, such as a mistaken strategy or being undone by his personal weaknesses. Sometimes, also, lack of self-confidence, sloppiness, or a poor recruitment may lead to failure.

Anyone who is uncovered should, however, drop suspicious objects in order to divert attention. During flight, leave behind objects that arouse doubt. This is something that needs to be skillfully managed, as such things will surely be subjected to severe scrutiny. It is very important to be aware of this. Letters of defamation or falsified clues that can cast doubts about other individuals among those in the shinobi's entourage are not rare.

When the shinobi stands up as a witness and shifts his own transgressions onto others, he can escape his persecutors. This is an infamous method but an effective one. Although there are a large number of strategies of this kind, they offer themselves on a case-by-case basis and are consequently hard to describe. Using them knowingly can easily spare a shinobi suffering a drastic penalty.

Whatever a shinobi can make appear as if by magic should put him in the position of crafting a plan of great depth, which will cast people into fear and doubt.

The moment when it is necessary to proceed to investigations should be recognized and taken seriously.

8

THE ART OF BRINGING TRUE INTENTIONS TO LIGHT

(*HITO NI RI O TSUKUSA SURU NARAI NO KOTO*)

————◄ ►————

Hito ni ri o tsukusa suru is the art of knowing how to behave around others. Someone who is empty himself grasps the principle* and can obtain information from another individual when that person is incautious. In order to do this, the key consists in daring to chat, spreading absolutely futile information while waiting to learn the true intentions of others. To collect someone's true intentions, you must create a void within yourself, not speak of what interests you personally but allow other people to speak and slowly draw near to their real intentions.

If this process should need to last for days, it is necessary to flatter the person, which will arouse his pride and the signs described earlier will then be recognized. When you pursue a conversation after these first signs have appeared, the true intentions of the interlocutor will be made immediately visible. At this time, the shinobi should not relax his attention

———

*See introduction, page 21.

but continue the conversation; otherwise any advantage he has gained will be lost. It is important for him to hide his true intentions so as not to reveal anything but unimportant information about himself.

Using personal modesty and restraint, the shinobi will cause men to reveal their intentions clearly. When someone maintains a state of emptiness while maintaining good relations with others, it is always easier to recognize their intentions. This is why it is so important to be able to leave your ego to the side. In order to be a truly effective spy, it is extremely important to be completely empty. Using others and manipulating them without their knowledge, while deftly flattering them without seeking to force anything at all, is an extraordinary notion that needs to be understood in its entirety.

9

RECOGNIZING AN INDIVIDUAL'S CHARACTER

(*NINSO O SHIRU KOTO*)

◄►

There are methods for observing people that will allow you to indubitably recognize how they think as well as their character. It is said that the Self listens to the heart attentively, so observing the heart allows you to see and read that of the other like your own image in a mirror. He whose heart is not serene can quickly fall victim to others. This is why the shinobi uses this technique and is able to follow his adversary's heart anywhere and penetrate it.

This is the foundational technique of the shinobi.

You should first study the position of the person's body and its movements, his art and manner of talking, the tone of his voice, and finally the color of his face and his behavior.

An enormous wealth of information can be gained from observing the three parts of the face.* The top part of the face extends from the hairline to the eyebrows. If this part of the face is elongated, the person can count on a long and happy

---

*See introduction, page 17.

life. The middle part extends from the eyebrows to the base of the nose. If this part is elongated, it can be described as the sign of a very noble character. The bottom part extends from the nose to the chin. If this part is elongated, it can be interpreted as the sign of a miserable character.

Men and women should not be examined differently, but if men reveal an aggressive nature by their foreheads or voices, this is indicative of poor character.

10

THE THREE ZONES
OF THE HUMAN BODY
(*MOTTAI NI SANTEI ARU KOTO*)

————◄ ►————

The head is considered to be the top zone. If it is large, it is not regarded as a sign of poor character but it is seen as indicating a short life. Rather, poor character is revealed by a small head. Other signs of poor character are unsteady knees, narrow hips, and a downward-curving mouth.

When speaking of the middle zone, we are referring to the region that extends from the shoulders to the hips. If this region is short, it indicates a short life and a lack of will. If the middle part is shorter than the legs, this is a sign by which a lack of self-confidence can be recognized. Women who have straight shoulders usually have no friends and are often desperate for a man.

We name the space that extends from the hips to the feet the bottom zone. If this area is longer than the middle part, this means that the person is prone to illness and undoubtedly comes from other provinces. When a woman smiles, covers her mouth with her hand, emphasizes her eyebrows, or casts glances to the side when she meets someone in such a way that only half her face is visible, it means she is either a prostitute or an artist. If the bones of her body are prominent, it means she has a miserable character.

It is a positive sign when the relationship between the three zones of the body is harmonious. A poor character can be recognized by disproportionate sizes in this regard. A cultured and well-educated character and a long life are indicated by a round and fleshy head, thin lips and white teeth, beautiful well-formed and full ears, a narrow nose, a stark contrast between the white and black of the eyes, handsome, long eyebrows, a large round belly, a handsome back, sloping shoulders, and a large, flat chest. While walking, the posterior should not sway nor jut out in a prominent manner, otherwise it brings to mind a person of a petty-minded nature.

All of the following are signs for a long and prosperous life: having a gleam or clear light in the eyes and eyelids that do not droop; not holding the head on the side when looking at something, even just a quick glance; not having any impurities in the eye colors; not having an angry or threatening presence, and adopting a dignified attitude, whether standing or sitting down. It is as if you are paddling through the waves while on board a large boat, and, despite the increasing roughness of the waves, retaining an unshakable courage. Although you may have worries and anxieties, you should not give up completely. Whoever carries this in himself will enjoy a long, rich life.

The following are all indications of a character that is similar to that of a bodhisattva: a silhouette that shines out in the most beautiful form without the slightest impurity; a strong voice that can be heard faraway, an unflappable mind, tall stature, a large forehead with narrow eyebrows, elocution unaccompanied by any gestures, resembling a mountain when seated, not allowing the body to stand out because of a strong odor; long tongue; long, slender fingers; hands that hang relaxed upon the hips; hair on the heels; or a birthmark.

The signs of wealth are: speaking in a sustained tone with a single breath, and having large shiny teeth and a navel deep enough to hide a date inside it. A rich person has soft skin, does not gorge when eating, and does not move his head when he swallows.

A person with a lot of hairs in the ears and nose, a clear mind, good height, strong muscles, supple veins, a full voice, harmonious cheeks, long hairy ears, long white eyebrows, a long occiput, smooth palms, and the back of whose heels are fleshy will enjoy a long and happy life.

To the contrary, the following attributes indicate a truly poor character: crab eyes and an expression of uncertainty; the person cries when laughing, and displays an impure face covered with blotches, a deformed auricle, and short hairs, although covered with hair.

A man of low extraction will not open his eyes when sleeping and will have a cold head. It is also said that a modest individual has a birthmark in the eyebrows and weak legs, and that a head that sags is a sign of infidelity.

THE HEAD

Good character can be recognized by well-proportioned and symmetrical cheeks, full jaws that fill out the face and that do not create lantern jaws. If both sides of the chin end in two horns and what is called "the happiness bone" sticks out behind the ears like a tiny horn, this can be considered to be a sign of longevity. If the head is round and shiny, the individual will find professional happiness in high positions. White hair that turns black toward the back is generally regarded as an auspicious sign. People with fine, black hair will follow an official, professional path as their career. Long thick hair and a hollow at the nape of the neck betray a petty-minded nature. Someone with a cowlick is skeptical by nature.

THE EYEBROWS

Fine eyebrows that are flat and shiny are a good sign. It is a particularly auspicious sign if a birthmark is placed in the eyebrows. Eyebrows that sit high on the forehead are the mark of a high professional post, and white hairs in the eyebrows are the heralds of a long life. If the hairs of the eyebrows point upward, the person is rich, and if they are gleaming, he is wise. If they grow lengthwise beyond the eyes, the person is particularly honest and loyal, and if the eyes are shaped like the sign *ichi,** this shows his sincerity toward his lord. Evil individuals have narrow eyebrows and deep orbits, and people prone to lying have sparse eyebrows. Drooping eyebrows are not a rarity among weak individuals.

---

*Japanese ideogram designating the number 1 (—).

THE EYES

Elongated, deep, and shining eyes denote a character of high worth, just as gleaming black lacquered eyes are the sign of a man of spirit. People with long narrow eyes most often enjoy long lives. A birthmark beneath the eye is the sign of a well-nourished individual. If the sign ichi can be recognized beneath the eyes, this is evidence of a princely character. Bad people have triangular eyes; if the corners of the eyes are drooping, it is a sign of a broken heart. Cold eyes are signs of hypocrisy and a swindler's nature.

THE NOSE

If the tip of the nose is prominent and rounded, it is the sign if a happy life and a cheerful character, and if the nose shows no particularity, that is also a good sign. An elongated, stiff, or high nose denotes good character, and if it is straight, it is a sign of loyalty. When the top part of the nose is narrow and it expands toward the bottom, this person will have many descendants. If someone's nose looks like a piece of split bamboo, he will certainly hold a high post and have a lot of money. If a birthmark is located on the upper part of the nose, the person concerned will have many male children whereas a person with one on the lower part will have mainly daughters. If a man should have a birthmark on the upper and lower part of his nose, he shall have two children. If his *jinchu** point is large and soft, this person has not yet lost a

---

*A well-known vital point in martial arts practice, located between the upper lip and the nose.

child. If a person has a wrinkle on one wing of the nose, it is a sign of an accident involving a team of horses. A long nose indicates an insensitive heart. If a person's nose looks like a beak, this individual has already killed people.

THE EAR

It is an auspicious sign when the ears are long and thick. A beautiful contour and a lobe pulling toward the mouth are signs of long life and financial success. Hair growing in the ears is a sign of longevity, and birthmarks there indicate a wise nature and a childhood in a good home. Reasonable, sensible people with a keen sense of humanity and justice have a large auricle entrance and elongated lobes. Someone whose ear is shaped like a kanji will be famous. Idiots and petty-minded people have ears that are dirty and neglected. Poor people's ears are somewhat similar to those of mice: located a little bit higher than eye level. Orphans and liars can be recognized by their ears with no curves and large openings.

THE MOUTH

A large, wide mouth is indicative of high position. Only a functionary of high rank and enjoying a long life span will be as tall as a bow and have red lips. Men with red, thick lips will be lucky and never suffer for want of food or clothing. Men who have a mouth shaped like the symbol *yon** are quite

---

*Japanese ideogram for the number 4 四, also pronounced as *shi*.

wealthy. Men with thick lips and a straight tongue have an instinct for seizing opportunities that bring happiness, and those with a thick tongue and a clear voice are well groomed and distinguished. People with a dark red tongue and a smile that does not show their teeth have an upper-class character.

Pointed and inverted mouths are signs of lower-class individuals. If the lips of a person move without emitting any sound, this is a sign that individual will die of hunger. Someone whose mouth looks like that of a mouse will speak badly of others and envy them. Lips that look like those of a person preparing to blow on a fire testify to a base character, and someone whose mouth resembles the chops of a dog will starve to death.

THE TEETH

Large, long teeth that sparkle and are deeply set are a good sign. People holding positions of high authority have teeth they do not reveal to the outside. Kings have thirty-eight teeth, the nobles of the court have thirty-six, and sages have more than thirty-four. People enjoying a life of ease have more than thirty and the rabble have only twenty-eight. If someone has teeth resembling those of Fukurokuju,* this heralds a long and pros-perous life. If their teeth are pointed, they hold elevated rank, and if they resemble grains of rice, it can be sure they shall enjoy long life. A scholar of scripture will have dark lips and a white

---

*In Japanese folklore, Fukurokuju is one of the seven gods of happiness, inspired by the beneficial deities of Chinese tradition. He is the god of wealth, wisdom, virility, and longevity. He is depicted as an old bald man with a very long head and a white beard.

tongue and teeth. A heatless man will have teeth that protrude and liars will also have similarly prominent teeth, which turn inward.

THE TONGUE

A long, straight tongue is an auspicious sign. If a person can touch his nose with his tongue, he will attain high rank in court. A large, hard tongue belongs to special people. If it is bright red, this is a unique distinguishing feature. A narrow, long tongue, to the contrary, is evidence of the degeneration that is specific to liars. If the tongue is short and pointed, the individual will be tenacious and more grasping.

THE HAND

A sympathetic and compassionate individual who is not avaricious has long, narrow hands. If his arms naturally hang alongside his body, reaching the top of the knee, this is a sign of an experienced individual. If a person's hands do not reach the top of his hips when dangling along his sides, it denotes a shameless and miserable life. A man of strong stature whose fingers are fragile at their ends is, in truth, poor but pure in spirit and can be satisfied making do with little. If the insides of someone's hands are clammy and give off a bad smell, then he is a poor and wretched individual.

Long, slender fingers belong to a sage, and anyone of high intelligence will have long, thick palms. A rich individual has palms whose outer edges are fleshy and have a hollow in the middle. A man of character and high rank has deep and well-defined lines on his palms. It is very auspicious if these lines are handsome and straight, and resemble a kanji. If they extend up to his fingers, a man can obtain everything he desires. An intelligent and experienced character is revealed by finely sketched lines that intersect. People who are modest, rich, wise, of high rank, and are famous have lines on their palms in which the following ideograms can be recognized:

十 丗 丗 井 人 灸 卓 叒 叕 皿 巛 土
火 又 开 丁刀 彡 巛 口

Thick fingernails are a beneficial sign and, if they are sparkling, they belong to a sensible individual who is steadfast in his thought. A person who is greedy and poor, to the contrary, will have short, thick fingernails.

BIRTHMARKS

It is unpleasant to have a birthmark where it can always be seen, but it is a good sign when it is placed in a concealed spot. A mark on the *indo** point is the identifying feature of a wise and strong man, and a person with a mark on the *sasho*

---

*The *indo* point is equivalent to the *choto* point, located almost exactly between the two eyes, above the bridge of the nose (the famous third eye). Like jinchu, it is an *atemi* point that is highly regarded and familiar to martial arts practitioners. This is only my personal hypothesis, but couldn't the author have been seeking to provide some clues about the location of vital points under the cover of discussing physiognomy?

(the *sasho* is left of the *tengaku,* which is itself placed left of the *tenchu**), will obtain high positions but will also lose his parents at an early age.

A well-tempered character can be recognized by a birthmark on the sole of the feet and the individuals possessing one have a great deal of luck in difficult situations. If someone has a birthmark on the upper part of the thigh, he shall seek to obtain high posts, and if it is located on the left side, this will be a sign of wealth and stability for one who follows the career path of a functionary. Wealthy and wise individuals have a mark beneath the navel.

A red-and-black blend at the edges of the birthmark is evidence of a petty-minded nature. A birthmark on the left side of the belly announces a death by drowning, birthmarks around the ears are the sign of a body tortured by pain, and those who have one on the jinchu point are people who hate living alone.

DECODING HUMAN CHARACTER

The doctrine for reading human character is detailed, flawless, and above reproach. The purpose of these notes is to draw up an inventory of characteristics bestowed by birth. Yet sometimes mistakes have been made. Although, for example,

---

*The *tenchu* point is located in the upper end of the median line crossing the face vertically, just at the top of the forehead, a little in front of the hairline. As indicated here, the *tengaku* point is located quite close to it on the left, as is the *sasho* point.

a person's character may appear completely evil, it can happen that he has some good aspects and should not be stigmatized because of some bad character features.

Predicting the good and evil in an individual is a difficult undertaking that must be approached with finesse. If the shinobi is experienced, recognizing what the individual wants does not present a problem. However, seeking to know the character of someone without having looked them in the eyes is a flawed approach. A shinobi must master the art of easily decoding an individual's true character.

PART FOUR

Shoninki Gekan

FINAL SCROLL
OF THE *SHONINKI*

1

THE MOST SECRET PRINCIPLES
(*GOKU HIDDEN*)

———◄ ►———

Within ninjutsu is the principle of *senpenbanka*,* which postulates that everything is subject to constant change and transformation. The essence of this principle is impossible to grasp in a single study. It is important to know a land, its particular places, and the feelings of its inhabitants. The purpose and duty of a shinobi should be to skillfully blend into them so they can be used to his best advantage. You penetrate men's hearts† and the highest principles when

---

*The literal meaning of *senpenbanka* is "one thousand transformations and ten thousand changes." This principle can be likened to the Buddhist notion of impermanence. Its corollaries are the principles concerning adaptation and movement. This expression is used in relation to combat techniques. When a practitioner has mastered a technique by grasping the profound sense of a move or a grip, he can then do it senpenbanka—use it in all its forms and variations, adapting it to any situation, and finding multiple applications for it.

†We should not forget that the word *heart* is symbolic and is a translation here for the Japanese *shin* or *kokoro*. The term *heart* is a key element throughout the entire book, in which it should be read and understood as "soul," "spirit," or "feeling;" the phrase *state of heart* should thus be translated as "state of being," "inner state," or "state of mind."

you cross through the "gateless barriers" (*mumon no isseki*). Then all knowledge becomes clear.

I cannot explain here the secret of the soul with these words. However, if the shinobi learns this knowledge, it will attain its fullness in the four directions of Heaven and, folded back upon itself, will find a place in his heart. This extremely important knowledge integrates the mysteries of the universe and the most uncustomary things, and sheds light in the most extraordinary fashion upon the course of time. This is the path for learning everything without effort.

What is transmitted below are the preliminary conditions for understanding the secret principles of ninjutsu. However, the shinobi should not stick too strictly to the written words; he will be able to understand them by pursuing his study of the hearts of men.

2

THE "GATELESS BARRIER"

(*MUMON NO ISSEKI*)

I t is hard to sound the human heart. If you draw near it, the person will hide it without hesitating. This is why it is advisable to talk about ordinary life, going deeper little by little, and exploiting the presumption of the adversary.

Grab the thread and do not let go.

To get to the bottom of the hearts of enemy spies, it is necessary to know their ambitions and intentions. If the other person is suspicious, it is essential to hide your own intentions completely. To achieve this objective, you should connect with the adversary's heart and ask questions without letting up. If you are questioned, you should talk about unimportant local matters in complete innocence while at the same time scrutinizing the heart of your adversary. As the saying goes:

> During interrogation, you should not give any ground
> And when you talk, you should let nothing filter through.

These are unquestionably wise words. If you are seeking to gain access to certain information, you must introduce similar themes in order to find a way in. It is not advisable to make too many waves. Minor and trivial facts should be known so you can question the other person about the subject.

The principles that a person's own heart has not birthed will continually change in content; then the person will align themselves with outside influences. An expert can constantly penetrate into a stranger's heart without being noticed and thereby cross the barrier that has no gate.

If a shinobi meets other men, he should always work kuruma ni kakuru, as taught by our school, which consists of spying upon the enemy's heart without exciting notice and without arousing suspicion. If the shinobi is still inexperienced, the greatest prudence is required when he falls into the snare of the adversary. He must have the presence of mind to exploit every small advantage and learn how to quickly recognize and use all his foe's weaknesses. This is what an old song teaches us:

At the break of day, attention slackens
Because he who is still looking at the moon in the sky
Will open the door to his heart and during this
  brief moment
The moon will still shine just as long as the time it
  takes to say so.

Indeed, you should never allow your own attention to wander.

3

THE ART OF NOT BREAKING INDIVIDUALS

(*HITO O YABURAZARU NO NARAI*)

◄►

Destroying a man detours us away from the objective we are working to achieve. If we are animated by rage, we lose our advantage. It is by following worldly principles that we become arbitrary and things become difficult. Consequently, there are eras during which the individual is subject to oppression and others in which we should rebuild. This is something that is hard to explain in words. Yet it is important to take into account.

The notion of force can be classified as hard, flexible, strong, and weak. Whoever is incapable of making these distinctions will harden his heart when everything is calling for sensitivity, and make the mistake of exhibiting his strength when it is necessary to show proof of weakness.

Becoming the enemy (*teki ni naru*) means putting yourself in the place of the other person and, in this way, taking a sounding of his heart. Sounding the heart is a wonderful thing: it is first necessary to observe in order to apply the appropriate strategy. This is an exact equivalent to the immutability of the *tenchijin,** which ensures it is cold in winter and hot during the summer. When a shinobi is cold, other people will also be cold. The adversary also knows his point of view quite well. This is why it is necessary to deeply examine those people who want to be like you. "Taking the enemy's heart" (*teki no kokoro o toru*) means judging his reaction when you have ensnared him and, in this way, "taking his heart." This is a well-thought-out strategy belonging to the technique of becoming the enemy (*teki ni naru*), and for that reason should be definitely taken into account.

The Meaning of *Tenchijin* in Ninjutsu

In the expression *tenchijin* (Heaven-Earth-Man), Heaven, Earth, and Man symbolize the totality of the universe, engendered by the interaction of all the elements that are included therein. This is a concept equivalent to the "Three" who are the origin of the "ten thousand beings," which symbolized the entire universe in the Chinese Taoist tradition, as expressed by Lao Tzu: "A source emerged, long before the birth of Heaven and Earth, nameless and hidden; knowing not its name, I called it Tao. The Tao produced the One, the one produced the Two, the Two produced the Three, the Three produced the ten thousand beings."

However, for some commentators, this expression in the distinctive context of ninjutsu could also be interpreted

---

*An expression that literally means "Heaven-Earth-Man" (*ten-chi-jin*).

as a coded abbreviation of the art of the ninja, classifying its three primary means of action:

Ten, designating atmospheric conditions in the broad sense and that the ninja should know how to use to his advantage (for example finding his way using the stars for direction, or knowing how to use a rainy night to conceal infiltration)

Chi, designating nature, which the ninja uses for hiding and surviving (knowing how to find food in the wild, for example), or the environment in the broad sense, such as material objects

Jin, meaning the human element, which can refer to when the ninja melts into the populace to hide, or the knowledge of how to corrupt or manipulate an individual, or to his knowledge of how to use all the resources offered by his body and mind

---

Finally, freeing oneself of the adversary (*teki ni hanaru*) means having the viewpoint of the adversary in such a way that you remain yourself as well. The advantage of this perspective is that everything is subject to change and is constantly varying. Whoever wishes to triumph using this strategy must definitely be an expert, because there are strong changes, despite everything, that can be missed while employing this ruse.

Someone who is looking for an advantage and who resorts solely to the strategies described above will only remain a novice, both before and after. However, being able to separate from someone and meet up with him later, because the lat-

ter personally revealed his travel itinerary without even having been directly questioned on the matter, is an exceptional
performance.

In this way, you can break a powerful foe into pieces as
well as deceive an experienced enemy. To attain this high level
of performance, the shinobi must work on himself without
ceasing.

4

THE EMOTIONAL STATES

(*SHINSO NO KOTO*)

◄ ►

This is a point of major importance. In order to learn how to interpret different facial expressions, it is necessary to know all the emotions of the heart. If you solely use human physiognomy in your evaluations, you will make mistakes. But if a shinobi manages to penetrate the emotional states of the heart, he will no longer commit any errors.

Start by learning your own heart, which was granted to you by Heaven, and learn to know it well. Meditate on all its aspects, then compare them with those of other men.

THE SEVEN STATES OF THE HEART

We make a distinction between seven emotional states that are inherent in every person's heart (*shichijo*):

1. Joy (*yorokobu*). Seeking joy is the primary emotion of the heart.
2. Anger (*ikaru*). This is also an original emotion.

3. Sorrow (*kanashimu*). This is the original emotion of all beings endowed with sensation.

4. Pleasure (*tanoshimu*). The soul greatly longs for everything that will give it pleasure.

5. Love (*ai*). Love is a primary emotion.

6. Hate (*nikumu*). A character with a strong penchant for evil is very uncommon.

7. Desire (*musaboro*). This is an original tendency that is deeply rooted in everyone's soul.

In Buddhist doctrine there are seven similar concepts: joy (*ki*); anger (*do*); sorrow (*hi*); will (*shi*); pain (*yu*); fear (*kyo*); wonder (*kyo*).

These emotional states are not fully formed when a person is born. All seven of these states are only fully formed at birth when the individuals involved are bodhisattvas. The seven emotions change in tandem with each other as a person grows older, depending on the circumstances of the individual's life; they mutually influence each other's development. While one of these states may prevail over the other six as a result of changes in the environment or the flow of time, giving rise to what is generally spoken of as the person's character, the others will be present also.

The seven emotional states are subject to the principle of ceaseless change (*senpenbanka*). For example, acquiring property or rising in rank and status, accumulating gold and money, and countless other things will bring joy to a person's heart. It is extremely difficult, though, to discern the exact causes for the feeling of joy. Similarly, let's take the emotion of anger. It can surge during combat, when having a conflict with another person, following a loss, or from feeling bitterness toward the world. It is, therefore, truly quite difficult to say with certainty what the real origin of that anger might be because the individual is no longer in a state to say anything objective about it and only that emotion alone is visible on his face.

Although the causes of emotion may appear to be identical, one should be mindful of the fact that there can be differences between them as great as the distance that separates Heaven and Earth. This is something you must study thoroughly. There are numerous hidden meanings and vast knowledge on this subject is something that can only be passed on orally (*okuden*).

5

KNOWING HOW TO TELL THE DIFFERENCE BETWEEN KNOWLEDGE AND PRINCIPLE

(DORI TO RIKO TO SHIRUBEKI KOTO)

———————

What we call principle is what is permanent. It is immutable essence. Growing in knowledge is certainly of value, but knowledge is subject to ceaseless change. The fundamental principle, to the contrary, is not quantifiable, and when studied attentively, makes everything clear. It is more important than knowledge, which can cast a shadow on clarity. This point is discussed here for the benefit of the reader.

The principle is similar to a sound that is heard by the ear. Even if there is an obstacle on its path, the sound will continue traveling along its path unchanged until reaching the ear. The strength of principle resides in the fact that its essence remains unchanged even if it travels a distance of many ri.*

———————

*Here the use of *ri* (previously mentioned as an old Japanese unit of measurement) is purely symbolic and simply conveys the idea of a vast distance.

Knowledge is like an object seen by the eye. If a sheet of paper is placed in front of the eyes, it becomes impossible to see that object. Furthermore, the words of knowledge change when they travel from place to place; this is why people should be aware that knowledge is subject to constant change.

Consequently, it should be realized that principle leads to authentic understanding while knowledge is an illusion. When you instill calm in your heart, the words you speak will be wonderful. When feelings pop up suddenly and disrupt reason, knowledge will become confused first of all, then the principle will become distorted, making the essence of things even harder to discern. This is a snare that you must therefore elude.

6

CONTROLLING YOUR HEART AND ATTAINING THE PRINCIPLE

(*KOKORO NO OSAME RI NI ATERU KOTO*)

————▶————

The shinobi controls his heart when he no longer permits feelings to invade it, develops appropriate energy, and leaves things devoid of meaning to the side. He must be constantly encouraging his own progress and thereby building himself a solid foundation. Anyone who is impatient will draw difficulties down on his head when spying. Whoever neglects the cultivation of his mind will exhaust his emotionally burdened heart and increase his risks of failure.

A calm, relaxed heart gives us the ability to effortlessly and continually decipher the innermost recesses of the hearts of men, even those that are unknown, and to track down their intentions. Such a heart will also allow us to endure even the most intolerable hardships and destroy the most blatant doubts with the help of strong thoughts and a vigorous mind. We should aspire to have a relaxed and robust heart.

There is nothing mysterious about the human heart. It is endowed with the five universal elements: wood, fire, earth, metal, and water,* which reveal themselves but briefly. While it is possible to explain the life of the heart, the reason for its existence will be much harder to find. With the strength of your own heart it is possible to give warmth to what is cold and to cool down without water what is hot. It is possible to make wood echo, cause water to emerge from metal, and bring about the birth of life in the earth.

The way the heart can adapt to everything is wonderful! Fire, which by itself has no will, will spread and burn on the whim of circumstance. Wood, whether large or small, will take root and reproduce in accordance with environmental circumstances. Wind will strike down the wooden tree and cause its leaves to spin in a wild dance. Anything that obstructs its course will be pitilessly destroyed. Although metal is regarded as a hard material, it changes shape when worked on by man.

Anyone who does not understand the principle of the five elements will naturally be incapable of speaking about them and will only be able to master the techniques of a shinobi in a mediocre way at best.

---

*See introduction, page 13.

7

THE ART OF FREE CONVERSATIONS

(*MUKEI BENZETSU*)

It is said that there is no special, established way for speaking for a shinobi. The tongue adapts to time and circumstances. You should be able to abandon a plan or preconceived idea without hesitation. During critical or dangerous moments, it is particularly important to be flexible in reacting to the changes made by the enemy. When the heart is clear, you can act in a way adapted to unanticipated situations without having to reflect more deeply on the principle that embraces everything.

Originally, shinobi and bushi were placed on the same level, but in no way did this include bandits or night burglars. This is why the leaders of the shinobi clan had already made names for themselves in the past, and leadership of the group was entrusted to those who displayed the greatest capability. In particularly important or dangerous cases, the high chiefs of the clans would take personal responsibility for this charge. During that era, they could not attach any importance to their own lives.

A proverb says, "Life is included in death, just as death is included in life; it is therefore important to free oneself from both life and death, which can be compared to a double-edged sword."

An ancient poem teaches us:

> *Similar to the empty carapace of the*
> *cicada,*
> *The body becomes an empty shell.*
> *I am no longer terrified*
> *If that should prove to be my fate, too.*

Someone unable to detach himself will be troubled and diverted from his purpose. But he who manages to free himself promptly and in time will no longer have anything to fear. He will then be able to clearly examine what he has undertaken. Even if, in a fit of rage, a man breaks objects, he will be liberated and able to act while forgetting himself (*muga mushin*).

An even more exact explanation of this can be expressed as the enforcement of Buddhist principles so strongly that you would lose yourself like an aspirant for illumination. When a shinobi recognizes the highest principles, he can put life and death in perspective and accept them.

Entering the "void"* when you are being hunted, being

---

*This is a translation of the word *ku,* which has two meanings. Its primary meaning is "the void," synonymous with "vacuum" or "nothingness." However, in Japanese thought, all is present in potential in the void, and all phenomena and objects have their origins there. Consequently, ku is also the fundamental and subtle essence of all things. As such, the void is considered as a complete element unto itself, just like air or fire, and is thereby integrated into the Japanese gorin, as seen above. In this case, it could also be translated as "ether," as conceived in ancient and medieval physics.

invisible, and striving to achieve your goal while forgetting yourself, these are the secret principles of ninjutsu. To achieve this, all that is required is for you to simply contemplate and recognize your own destiny and self.

8

KNOWING HOW TO LET GO

(*RIJUTSUHO*)

———◄ ►———

It is advisable to not occupy yourself with several things at one time. When things become complicated, it stems from the fact that a shinobi has been unable to free himself through his own means, and has become entangled in his own plans. This is the reason why our own feelings and intentions must be put in balance with the essence of things, so that they do not sow confusion. In this way, the high principles will be clear to each and every one one of us and it will no longer be possible for anything to become cause for surprise.

When someone feels a strongly disproportionate fear in the presence of an enemy, he will be unable to penetrate his intentions. An expert will place his impressions and feelings to the side. When he then examines the adversary's heart, he will be able to read it and decipher his intentions. Just like the falcon dancing in the air can spot the bird trembling with fear beneath him, the shinobi spies upon and even pursues his adversary with one heart and one body undivided. For this reason we call this strategy *hicho no kirai*.

Under no circumstances should a shinobi ever be impatient. Should he fall victim to an error, he would no longer be capable of doing anything well. From this wound, errors will multiply in his heart like a forest of thorn trees. It is difficult to wait for a fruit to be ripe while it is still hanging from the branch. But if you act too hastily, it will only be half-ripe, and if you act too slowly, it will lie rotting upon the ground. You must seize the exact moment.

When the enemy is right in front of you face-to-face and unarmed, it is possible to talk with him. Made careless by this fact, a shinobi can then draw closer and engage him with *shinmyoken*.* Killing a person without using a sword and poisoning without poison are important possibilities offered by conversation. When the heart is strong, a person can walk atop the blades of swords or race over ice-covered hills. These are techniques of the heart.

Truly grasping the art of the shinobi—made possible by reading this treatise—will permit you to live without enemies and to have prosperous descendants.

---

*[*Shinmyoken* means "divine sword," so named because it involves overpowering an opponent without injuring him with a sword. —*Trans.*]

SHONINKI OKUSHO

▸ ►

I am not part of the path whose contents are described in this treatise.

People associate the most extraordinary powers with the notion of shinobi. It is claimed that the shinobi can easily deceive people, which is demonstrated in the art of this school. That is why when I met a shinobi who never tried to hide anything from me and openly offered me the secret arts, I was happy to take the trouble to understand and learn their exact value. To do this, it was necessary to be both proud and modest. As I am not familiar with this book, it is difficult for me to provide a text at the end that is perfectly appropriate, but I shall make no efforts to hide the extent of my ignorance from people.

The *Shoninki* contains the most profound secrets of the ninjutsu school in their purest form. The teacher passes them on to only one disciple, and to no one else but him. In our time, though, they are sometimes taught to a few certain people, on serious demand. Despite all, prudence is called for here, as the corresponding faculties are hypothetical, and in no case should this text be shown to anyone without authorization.

NATORI HEISAEMON
WRITTEN DURING THE THIRD YEAR OF THE KANPO ERA,*
THE FIRST DAY OF THE SECOND MOON,
FOR WATANABE ROKUROSAEMON

---

*In 1743, as the Kanpo era lasted four years, from 1741 to 1744.

INDEX

Page numbers in *italics* refer to illustrations.

BOOKS OF RELATED INTEREST

Shaolin Qi Gong
Energy in Motion
by Shi Xinggui

The Spiritual Practices of the Ninja
Mastering the Four Gates to Freedom
by Ross Heaven

The Magus of Java
Teachings of an Authentic Taoist Immortal
by Kosta Danaos

Nei Kung
The Secret Teachings of the Warrior Sages
by Kosta Danaos

Aikido and Words of Power
The Sacred Sounds of Kototama
by William Gleason

The Last Lama Warrior
The Secret Martial Art of Tibet
by Yogi Tchouzar Pa

Iron Shirt Chi Kung
by Mantak Chia

Martial Arts Teaching Tales of Power and Paradox
Freeing the Mind, Focusing Chi, and Mastering the Self
by Pascal Fauliot

INNER TRADITIONS • BEAR & COMPANY
P.O. Box 388
Rochester, VT 05767
1-800-246-8648
www.InnerTraditions.com

Or contact your local bookseller